Heike Link · John S. Dodgson
Markus Maibach · Max Herry

The Costs of Road Infrastructure and Congestion in Europe

With 23 Figures
and 38 Tables

Physica-Verlag

A Springer-Verlag Company

Series Editors
Werner A. Müller
Martina Bihn

Authors
Dr. Heike Link
German Institute for Economic Research (DIW)
Königin-Luise-Str. 5
D-14195 Berlin, Germany

John S. Dodgson
Associate Director
NERA
15 Stratford Place
GB-London W1N 9AF, United Kingdom

Markus Maibach
INFRAS
Gerechtigkeitsgasse 20
CH-8002 Zürich, Switzerland

Dr. Max Herry
Büro Dr. Herry
Argentinierstr. 21
A-1040 Wien, Austria

ISBN 3-7908-1201-3 Physica-Verlag Heidelberg New York

Cataloging-in-Publication Data applied for
Die Deutsche Bibliothek – CIP-Einheitsaufnahme
The costs of road infrastructure and congestion in Europe; with 38 tables/Heike Link... – Heidelberg: Physica-Verl., 1999
(Contributions to economics)
ISBN 3-7908-1201-3

© Physica-Verlag Heidelberg 1999
Printed in Germany

The use of general descriptive names, registered names, trademarks, etc. in this publication does not imply, even in the absence of a specific statement, that such names are exempt from the relevant protective laws and regulations and therefore free for general use.

Softcover Design: Erich Kirchner, Heidelberg

SPIN 10718639   88/2202-5 4 3 2 1 0 – Printed on acid-free paper

The Costs of Road
Infrastructure and
Congestion in Europe

Contributions to Economics

Christoph M. Schneider
Research and Development Management:
From the Soviet Union to Russia
1994. ISBN 3-7908-0757-5

Bernhard Böhm/Lionello F. Punzo (Eds.)
Economic Performance
1994. ISBN 3-7908-0811-3

Lars Olof Persson/Ulf Wiberg
Microregional Fragmentation
1995. ISBN 3-7908-0855-5

Ernesto Felli/Furio C. Rosati/
Giovanni Tria (Eds.)
The Service Sector:
Productivity and Growth
1995. ISBN 3-7908-0875-X

Giuseppe Munda
Multicriteria Evaluation
in Fuzzy Environment
1995. ISBN 3-7908-0892-X

Giovanni Galizzi/
Luciano Venturini (Eds.)
Economics of Innovation:
The Case of Food Industry
1996. ISBN 3-7908-0911-X

David T. Johnson
Poverty, Inequality and Social
Welfare in Australia
1996. ISBN 3-7908-0942-X

Rongxing Guo
Border-Regional Economics
1996. ISBN 3-7908-0943-8

Oliver Fratzscher
The Political Economy of Trade
Integration
1996. ISBN 3-7908-0945-4

Ulrich Landwehr
Industrial Mobility and Public Policy
1996. ISBN 3-7908-0949-7

Arnold Picot/Ekkehard Schlicht (Eds.)
Firms, Markets, and Contracts
1996. Corr. 2nd printing 1997.
ISBN 3-7908-0947-0

Thorsten Wichmann
Agricultural Technical Progress and the
Development of a Dual Economy
1997. ISBN 3-7908-0960-8

Ulrich Woitek
Business Cycles
1997. ISBN 3-7908-0997-7

Michael Carlberg
International Economic Growth
1997. ISBN 3-7908-0995-0

Massimo Filippini
Elements of the Swiss Market for
Electricity
1997. ISBN 3-7908-0996-9

Giuseppe Gaburro (Ed.)
Ethics and Economics
1997. ISBN 3-7908-0986-1

Frank Hoster/Heinz Welsch/
Christoph Böhringer
CO_2 Abatement and Economic
Structural Change in the European
Internal Market
1997. ISBN 3-7908-1020-7

Christian M. Hafner
Nonlinear Time Series Analysis
with Applications to Foreign Exchange
Rate Volatility
1997. ISBN 3-7908-1041-X

Sardar M. N. Islam
Mathematical Economics of
Multi-Level Optimisation
1998. ISBN 3-7908-1050-9

Sven-Morten Mentzel
Real Exchange Rate Movements
1998. ISBN 3-7908-1081-9

Lei Delsen/Eelke de Jong (Eds.)
The German and Dutch Economies
1998. ISBN 3-7908-1064-9

Mark Weder
Business Cycle Models with
Indeterminacy
1998. ISBN 3-7908-1078-9

Tor Rødseth (Ed.)
Models for Multispecies
Management
1998. ISBN 3-7908-1001-0

Michael Carlberg
Intertemporal Macroeconomics
1998. ISBN 3-7908-1096-7

Sabine Spangenberg
The Institutionalised Transformation of
the East German Economy
1998. ISBN 3-7908-1103-3

continued on page 138

Preface

This book presents the results of the study „Infrastructure Capital, Maintenance and Road Damage Costs for Different Heavy Goods Vehicles in the EU" which was commissioned by the European Commission, DG VII. This study supported the preparation of the white book on transport infrastructure charging. The study has been conducted by an European consortium consisting of DIW (German Institute for Economic Research, project leader and responsible for the country reports for Germany, Belgium, the Netherlands, Luxembourg and Sweden), INFRAS (responsible for the country reports for Switzerland, Denmark, Portugal and Greece), Consultancy Dr. Herry (responsible for the country reports for Austria, Finland, France and Italy) and NERA (National Economic Research Associates, responsible for the country reports for the UK, Ireland and Spain). The project ran from November 1997 to March 1998 and was monitored by a steering committee with representatives of the EU-member states.

This book is dealing with the calculation of costs for road infrastructure and congestion and the allocation of these costs to vehicle types. It focuses on heavy goods vehicles. This is a topic of high relevance for transport policy both on the national and the EU-level with a long tradition of political and scientific debate. The study contains a comprehensive methodological comparison of existing models for calculating road capital values and capital costs and for allocating infrastructure costs to vehicle types. The study also discusses the issue of estimating marginal infrastructure costs and approaches for estimating the costs of road congestion. For the first time in Europe the impacts of different national approaches applied in EU-member states on the quantitative results and their comparabilty were studied in a quantitative approach. Based on these extensive analyses of methodologies the study provides empirical results for road infrastructure and congestion costs in the EU-member states and in Switzerland for the year 1994.

Both the political and scientific relevance of the topic and the innovative character of the study will recommend this book for transport politicians, academics and consultants.

Acknowledgements

This book could not have been written without the support of a large number of people. First and foremost we are grateful to the EC-Commission for funding our research. Furthermore, we thank all representatives of member countries who supported our research by providing information, studies and data and by discussing our findings. In particular we thank the members of the steering committee W. Weigand and K. Stanger (Bundesministerium für Wirtschaft und Verkehr, Austria), J. van de Kerkhof (Ministerie van Verkeer en Infrastructuur, Belgium), K.E. Andersen (Road Directorate Denmark), J. Haavisto (Ministry of Transport and Communications, Finland), J. Leveque (SETRA, France), R.P. Eisele and R. Scharschmidt (Bundesministerium für Verkehr, Germany), D. Kallistrophos and A. Livieraton (R.P., Greece), P. Cialdini (Ministry of Public Works, Italy), M. Rotondo and L. Ercoli (AISCAT, Italy), J. Morby and P. Liebetegger (Ministère des Transports, Luxembourg), R. Huyser and I. Smits-Vossen (Ministerie van Verkeer en Waterstraat, The Netherlands), T. Soussa (Ministère de L´Equipment, Portugal), A. Sanchez-Rey (Spanish National Road Administration, Spain), J. Izarzugaza (Ministerio de Fomento, Spain) and H. Swahn (SIKA, Sweden) for the workload done in preparation of the meetings and discussing the reports. We extend our thanks to a large number of people in national authorities, statistical offices, institutes and consultancies who contributed to our study with data, general information and useful comments.

Special thanks are due to Anja Spahn (DIW), who provided secretarial and layout support of constant high quality.

Contents

1 Introduction

In July 1998 the European Commission adopted the White Paper „Fair payment for infrastructure use: A phased approach to a common transport infrastructure charging framework in the EU" which proposes an European intermodal approach for infrastructure charges. However, introducing a harmonised European framework for infrastructure charges requires first of all quantitative knowledge on infrastructure costs, congestion costs and accident and environmental costs for all modes and all EU-countries.

With the infrastructure regulation from 1970, the EU created a first basis for harmonisation and data reporting as far as infrastructure-related costs are concerned. However, this guideline provides only minimal standards and gives no criteria regarding the construction of a harmonised data basis. In fact, the current situation of infrastructure costs is heterogeneous and the quality of data relatively poor. In most European countries, only information on aggregated revenues and expenditure is available. Actual cost calculations, e.g. capitalised expenditures as annual opportunity costs in the economic sense are lacking. To date, infrastructure cost and infrastructure cost-coverage calculations are only available for a few countries. The situation in the field of congestion costs and costs for accidents and environmental damages is even poorer than those for infrastructure in the narrow sense.

Against this background our study on road infrastructure and congestion costs was aimed to support the Commission by providing the necessary cost accounts. The project was addressed to achieve three goals:

- Firstly, to create a theoretically adequate and practicable common methodology for the calculation of infrastructure costs including congestion costs, in particular for heavy goods vehicles (henceforth HGV).

- Secondly, to provide quantitative knowledge on road expenditures (investment, maintenance and operation), on the capital value of the road network and on infrastructure costs. This was to be supplemented by a summary of existing estimates for congestion costs of road transport.

- Thirdly, to derive policy recommendations regarding the implementation of the proposed methodology, data requirements and updating procedures.

The study is structured as follows. Starting point is a review of the existing practice of infrastructure cost accounting and of estimating congestion costs in the EU member states and in Switzerland (chapter 2). Chapter 3 contains a comprehensive analysis of different methodological issues such as estimation of capital values and capital costs, cost allocation to vehicle types, estimation of marginal infrastructure costs and approaches for calculating congestion costs. Based on the findings summarised there, we suggest on the one hand a methodological approach for estimating infrastructure costs and congestion costs for our study. The empirical results of this approach are presented in chapter 4. On the other hand, the findings mainly of chapter 3 form the basis for recommendations towards a future harmonised approach and for formulating data requirements as well as further research needs (chapter 5).

2 State of the art

2.1 Review of infrastructure cost and expenditure accounts

This chapter summarises the existing practice in Europe regarding the elaboration of cost and expenditure accounts by type of vehicles. A detailed discussion of selected methodological issues such as estimation of capital values and cost allocation methods will be given in chapter 3.

2.1.1 General overview of the practice in Europe

The practice of road cost accounts in Europe is summarised in table 1. As can be seen from there, both the general approaches for road cost accounts and the estimation methods for single cost components used in Europe vary considerably and lead to a rather heterogeneous situation. The most important purpose in those countries which have elaborated more or less frequent road accounts is to gain information on the cost coverage by type of vehicle as a basis for possible tax adjustment or the introduction/increase of existing road user charges. However, the frequency and quality of data provided and the methodology used differ considerably.

Table 1 indicates that middle European and Scandinavian countries use quite sophisticated methods to estimate their annual road costs on an economic basis. These countries have a strong public interest to gain information on the costs caused by different vehicle types. In contrast to that, national road accounts in southern countries are not well developed or do not exist at all. There are several reasons which might explain these differences: One important issue is the legal state of infrastructure. As soon as parts of the road network are operated privately (such as motorways in Italy, France, Spain, Portugal, etc.), cost accounting is a private duty in order to derive consistent pricing schemes, while in countries with a high share of transit traffic and public road network structures (for example

Germany, Austria, Switzerland) the knowledge of cost causation and cost coverage by vehicle types/user groups is of political interest.[1]

Table 1: Practice of road infrastructure cost accounts[3] in Europe

Criteria	Description	Practice in the following countries
Regular road account	Regular calculation of costs (or expenditures) for different categories, Comparison with revenues, Calculation of cost coverage	Annually: D[1], UK, CH Periodical updates: D[2], A, DK, NL, IRL, E, F, SF, S No estimates available: B, L, P, GR,
HGV road account	Differentiation of costs (or expenditures) for vehicle categories	D, UK, A, DK, IRL, E, F, NL, S, SF, CH,
Expenditure accounts	No capitalisation of the road investments	D, UK, NL, IRL, E, F, S, SF, I, CH
Cost accounts: Estimation of capital costs	Capitalisation of road investments by using assumptions on life expectancies and interests	D, A, DK, S, SF, F, CH,
Cost/expenditure allocation to vehicle categories	Use of a specific method to allocate costs/expenditures to different vehicle categories, especially for HGV.	Own method: D, UK, A, DK, F, NL, S, SF, CH, Method from another country adopted: IRL, E,
Distinction between fixed and variable costs/ expenditures		D, DK, S, SF, F, I

[1] Frequently elaborated cost data. - [2] Annual expenditure data. - [3] Congestion costs will be treated in section 2.2.

Sources: Review of studies, carried out by DIW, INFRAS, HERRY, NERA.

2.1.2 Classifications

According to the EC-regulation 1108/70, EU-member countries are obliged to report their annual road expenditures and the vehicle-km driven by vehicle types. For compiling the expenditure data, the regulation requires the following differentiation:

- Expenditure categories:

  - Investments (New roads, enlargement, renewal)

  - Current expenditures (maintenance, operation)

---

[1]   However, the legal state of road infrastructure is not the only explanation. In Spain for example, only 1 % of the total road network is operated privately as toll motorways. Thus, given the 99 % share of remaining roads in public responsibility, a public interest in road costs should exist.

– General expenditures (administration)

- Road categories: The road categories for which expenditure data have to be reported differ from country to country[2]. In general, information is required for the following categories:

  – National motorways

  – State roads (trunk roads)

  – Regional roads (Provincial roads)

  – Communal roads

In addition, the regulation asks for information on the use of road infrastructure (vehicle-km) for the following HGV categories:

– Lorries (2, 3, 4 axles)

– Lorries with trailer (2-2 axles, 2-3 axles, 3-2 axles, 3-3 axles, others)

– Tractors with semitrailer (2-1 axles, 2-2 axles, 3-1 axles, 3-2 axles, others)

The classifications used for expenditure types and road categories in the existing road accounts in European countries are more or less in line with these requirements. However, since there are differences according to the institutional framework condition (for example: share of private and public-owned motorways) and the organisation of the network, the comparability of data is restricted.

In several countries, the breakdown of road expenditures by type of expenditure is more detailed in order to design and apply methods for cost allocation to different types of vehicles. This is true mainly for the specification of road maintenance expenditures (i.e. weight dependent expenditures like pavement maintenance, see chapter 3.4.2). Considerable differences between the national road accounts which use a special cost allocation method can be stated regarding the consideration and definition of vehicle categories. While the formation of categories (according to axles, weight classifications) is quite similar, the differentiation (number of categories) varies (see details in the chapters 3.2.4 and 3.4.2).

2.1.3 Estimation of capital values

There are only a few countries in Europe (Austria, Denmark, Finland, Germany, Sweden, Switzerland) which derive capital costs out of the estimation of road capital values using economic costs instead of expenditures. There are two main approaches:

---

[2] The regulation contains detailed distinctions of road types for Belgium, Germany, France, Italy, Luxembourg and the Netherlands.

- The perpetual inventory concept: In this concept the capital value is estimated based on time series for investment expenditures (at least 30 years). It is used in Germany, Denmark, Sweden and Switzerland.

- The synthetic method: Here, the basis for estimating the capital value is a road inventory by types of assets and the respective specific costs of replacement. Austria and Finland have applied this method.

Furthermore, in countries like Italy, France, Spain and Portugal where parts of the road network are operated privately, the capital value of these parts is based on entrepreneurial principles (asset´s value in balance-sheets of the motorway companies) and is hardly comparable with the capital value derived by using the perpetual inventory concept.

We will discuss these approaches and their differences more detailed in chapter 3.3. The interested reader will find there also a quantitative analysis of the impacts of model types and parameters on the level and structure of capital costs.

2.1.4   Cost allocation methods

Table 2 shows the most important methodological issues of the allocation procedures used in different countries. Most of the countries distinguish between fixed and variable (i.e. vkm dependent) costs and allocate these by using different equivalent factors (for example vkm, PCU-km, standard axles-km). The most important differences occur in the use of equivalent factors, in the split of weight-dependent cost categories and in the value of the factors applied. We will discuss these methodological details and compare the quantitative results of the different methods in the chapters 3.4.2 and 3.4.3.

2.1.5   Consequences for a harmonised method

According to this brief review we can distinguish mainly three groups of countries which are characterised by different degrees of data availability and the existence of more or less sophisticated methodologies.

Group 1:   *Countries with detailed data and sophisticated methodology*

Germany, Austria, Denmark, Sweden, France[3], Finland[3] and Switzerland

Although the applied methodology differs within these countries, the empirical country results of our study should be based on the

---

[3]   For France, there are capital values for parts of the road network available. There exists also a cost allocation method which is, however, only applied to expenditures. The situation is similar in Finland.

Table 2: Cost allocation methods in Europe

Country	Method used
Austria	- Regression analysis - Adaptation of the German method
Denmark	Differentiation of capital and running costs into: - Fixed costs, - Vehicle-km dependent costs - Space dependent costs - Weight dependent costs Use of specific weight and space factors by type of vehicle
France	Differentiation between fixed and variable expenditures Use of different allocation factors such as: - vkm - weight-vkm - standard axle-vkm
Germany	Differentiation between marginal costs and capacity costs Allocation of: 1. Marginal costs by AASHO-Road factor*vkm 2. Capacity costs by (speed-dependent) equivalent factor*vkm
Italy	Differentiation between marginal and capacity expenditures Use of different allocation factors such as: - vkm - axle-weight-km - standard-axle-km
Netherlands	Differentiation of investment expenditures and running expenditures into different sub-categories Use of different allocation factors such as: - vkm - PCU-km - axle load-km
Finland	Differentiation between fixed and variable expenditures Use of different allocation factors such as: - vkm - weight-factors
Sweden	Differentiation of fixed and variable expenditures into: - vkm-dependent expenditures - space- and speed-dependent expenditures (allocated by PCU-km) - weight-dependent expenditures (allocated by AASHO-factor-km)
Switzerland	Allocation of: 1. Weight dependent costs of new investment (estimated by percentages per road type) by weight-factors 2. Weight dependent costs for pavement and investive maintenance by axle-load-vkm 3. Capacity costs: 80% by vehicle-length *vkm 20% by vkm 4. Current costs by vkm
United Kingdom	Allocation of: 1. Capital expenditure: 15% by max. GVW-km, 85% by PCU-km. 2. Maintenance expenditure: further differentiated by types of expenditures, different allocation factors applied 3. Policing and traffic wardens: by vehicle-km.

Sources: Review of studies carried out by DIW, INFRAS, HERRY, NERA.

existing figures. The data from these countries can be used for sensitivity analyses applying different calculation methods to existing data sets.

Group 2:   *Countries with a good database, but no sophisticated methodology*

United Kingdom[4], the Netherlands[4], Italy, Ireland, Belgium and Spain.

Especially for the estimation of capital values, long time series on investment expenditures or detailed inventory information can be used to apply methods from the countries in Group 1.

Group 3:   *Countries with only sporadic estimates and no own methodology*

Luxembourg, Portugal, Greece

For these countries the database is not sufficient to calculate capital values or marginal costs in detail. Only rough estimations are possible.

Obviously, we have to deal with the classical dilemma of harmonising methodological issues: On the one hand, using national results with a very low degree of harmonisation (at least for those countries, where these results are available) guarantees that we produce results on an official basis. However, due to the underlying different methodologies, the results are not really comparable. On the other hand, applying a harmonised calculation method would require specific and detailed data for each country. Standardised data which meet these requirements are hardly available for all countries.

We will examine the methodological issues in different European countries within chapter 3 in detail. After this review, and based on the knowledge of existing data, we will come back to the problem of harmonisation and will suggest in chapter 5 a common methodological approach and the necessary steps for the future to apply this approach.

---

[4]   Although the UK has no estimation of capital costs, the allocation method for different types of expenditures is very sophisticated. This holds to some extent also true for the Netherlands.

2.2 Congestion cost studies

2.2.1 Introduction

Congestion arises when traffic is delayed because of the presence of other vehicles. The clearest manifestation of congestion occurs where traffic is stuck in traffic jams. However, even in the worst jams, traffic is usually moving slowly in a start-stop fashion. Consequently, a wider interpretation of congestion is that it occurs wherever traffic moves more slowly on an existing road than it were to do if traffic were at low levels. In this section of the report we provide a brief overview of different attempts to measure traffic congestion costs in Europe. In doing so we distinguish between the main different concepts of congestion that are measured in the most important studies.

2.2.2 The components of congestion costs

In order to measure congestion costs it is first necessary to identify the main components of congestion costs. These are as follows:

- additional travel time for the different vehicles in the traffic flow. It is possible to distinguish between different types of road user in a number of ways, but a useful split is:
  - car travellers on business;
  - car travellers making non-work (including commuting) trips;
  - drivers, and other occupants, of light and heavy goods vehicles; and
  - drivers and passengers on buses.
- additional fuel costs; and
- other increases in vehicle operating costs, including extra tyre wear, brake wear and use of lubricants.

It is usual to value travel time in the course of work, such as time spent by goods vehicle drivers, by reference to hourly wage costs. The value of travel time spent in non-work activities is normally valued using revealed preference or stated preference methods which consider the extent to which individuals are willing to pay to save time.

When these types of values are used, they generally show that around 90 per cent of the costs of congestion are accounted for by increased travel time, and the remainder by increased fuel and other operating costs. Consequently, it is particularly important to measure the impact of congestion in increasing journey times, and to value those increases in travel time correctly.

2.2.3 Alternative measures of congestion

In reviewing different studies of congestion costs, the most important distinction to make is that between studies which measure the total costs of congestion (and by implication, the average cost of congestion incurred by each vehicle in the traffic flow), and studies which measure the marginal cost of congestion. The marginal cost of congestion shows the extra congestion costs caused by an additional vehicle joining a traffic flow. This marginal cost of congestion will be zero if the traffic flow is not congested, but eventually as traffic flows rise congestion will occur, and then the marginal cost of congestion will rise as the flow increases towards the physical capacity of the road.

2.2.4 Studies of the total costs of congestion

There are two main approaches to the measurement of the total costs of traffic congestion. One approach uses a modelling framework in which actual traffic conditions are compared with hypothetical "free-flow" conditions. The alternative approach utilises data on actual traffic delays, often based on police reports. Since the latter approach is based on major reported delays and traffic jams, it is likely to yield rather lower estimates of the total costs of congestion than is the first approach.

As an example of the first approach, project team members NERA derived estimates of total congestion costs in Great Britain for the year 1996. These estimates were based on very detailed traffic flow data for the whole of the British road network for different times of the day or week. Total congestion costs were estimated by comparing the traffic speeds likely to be observed on each part of the network with the speeds which would be obtained if traffic were able to move freely. Differences in travel time were then valued using values of time for different types of vehicle, while increases in operating costs were measured using operating cost formulae which relate fuel and other operating costs per km to average traffic speed. Total congestion costs in 1996 were estimated at £7 billion (8.5 billion ECU).

Other studies using this type of traffic modelling approach to estimate traffic congestion costs have been carried out in Spain (for the city of Madrid), and in Ireland (for the city of Dublin).

Other studies of the total costs of congestion have considered the costs of traffic jams on particular types of road. In the Netherlands, the NEA (Transportonderzoek en-opleiding) have used traffic police reports of actual traffic jams to estimate delay costs on the main road network in the Netherlands. These estimates of increased time and fuel costs were then increased to allow for "situations tending towards a jam". Studies in other countries, including Germany,

Italy, and Switzerland have also considered congestion costs on particular types of roads which arise as a result of delays.

2.2.5 Studies of the marginal costs of congestion

Studies of the marginal costs of congestion consider the extra time, fuel and other operating costs that will be imposed on all existing vehicles in a traffic flow when an extra vehicle joins the flow. These marginal costs are therefore usually expressed as the additional costs per (extra) vehicle-km. Mayeres et al. (1996) have estimated marginal congestion costs in terms of extra time costs for the city of Brussels, following an increase in traffic flow at different periods of the day. Thus they project marginal congestion costs per extra vehicle-km in the year 2005 as 1.39 ECUs for a car in the peak, and 0.004 ECUs for a car in the off-peak. Marginal congestion costs for different types of vehicle in different types of traffic flow have also been estimated for France and for Sweden.

Table 3: Approaches for measuring congestion costs in Europe

Criteria	Description	Practice in the following countries
Total congestion cost studies based on modelling approach	Comparison of actual traffic conditions with „free-flow" situation	UK, IRL
Total congestion cost studies based on actual delay information	Data on actual traffic delays used	A, NL, I, E, CH[1]
Studies on marginal congestion costs		B, F, S
[1] Running study.		
Sources: Review of studies, carried out by DIW, INFRAS, HERRY, NERA.		

2.2.6 Conclusions on existing studies of congestion costs

In comparing studies of traffic congestion costs in different countries, it is important to note the different bases on which estimates are provided. Although we have identified studies for a number of Member States, the estimates of congestion costs may not be comparable because:

- some estimates are based on estimates of total congestion costs, though not necessarily for the whole of the road network, while some estimates are provided in terms of marginal congestion costs for different types of vehicle in different types of traffic flow; and

- some of the estimates of total costs are based on an analysis of traffic conditions throughout a country or a major city, while some of the estimates relate to major delays on particular types of road.

In chapter 3.6 we will explain the approach recommended in the present study. This approach involves considering estimates of the marginal costs of congestion, since it is marginal costs which are relevant for determining optimal use of capacity. It also involves adopting a harmonised approach to the measurement of marginal congestion costs across Europe.

3 Methodology

3.1 Methodological overview

The aim of this chapter is threefold. Firstly, it is necessary to clarify some definitions in order to guarantee a transparent communication of methodological issues. Secondly, the interrelations between infrastructure cost, congestion cost and pricing principles have to be explained. Thirdly, the different aims of infrastructure cost accounting have to be analysed regarding their methodological consequences.

3.1.1 Some definitions

In order to develop a consistent methodology, it is important to define the different cost components properly. The following distinctions are particularly important (see also the descriptions in the glossary):

- **Expenditures and costs**: Whereas expenditures are periodical (e.g. annual) monetary flows, cost figures consider the service life and opportunity cost (benefits of alternative use which were not realised) of investments. Thus, they reflect economic reality in respect to each period.

- **Investment expenditures and capital costs:** Capital costs are derived by capitalising investment expenditures for the road network. Expenditures with an expected lifetime of more than one year have to be capitalised (that means depreciation and interests have to be calculated).

- **Running expenditures and running costs:** Running expenditures for roads such as traffic police, operation of signalling and street lighting, snow sweeping, etc. are annual monetary flows with a lifetime of less than one year (production and consumption fall in the same period). They are not be capitalised and are consequently equal to the running costs.

- **Fixed and variable costs:** Fixed costs are equal to those costs, which are independent on the mileage driven, whereas variable costs depend on the use of road infrastructure. Parts of capital cost and running cost might be either fixed or variable. Therefore, it is important to hint at the fact that the terms fixed cost and capital cost and the terms variable cost and running cost cannot be used synonymously.

- **Average and marginal costs** are both specific costs per unit of output. Whereas average costs are defined as the total cost (fixed and variable) per unit of output, marginal cost are (mathematically) equal to the first derivative of total costs with respect to output. Marginal costs represent the additional cost of an additional vkm or an additional vehicle. They are not equal to variable costs but equal to the first derivative of total variable costs, while differentiating fixed costs yields zero.

- The shares of cost components which are considered to be variable or fixed depend on the time horizon. Consequently, with respect to the time horizon short-run and long-run marginal costs have to be distinguished:

  - **Short-run marginal costs** are related to the use of already existing infrastructure. Capacity is given and cannot be adjusted to changes of demand in the short-run. For uncongested roads marginal costs are equal to the additional deterioration of infrastructure and the consumption of other items caused by additional vehicles. For congested roads additional time and operating costs arise.

  - Theoretically, all production factors are variable in the long-run. Consequently, in this extreme case fixed costs do not exist. Given this general definition it can be stated that **long-run marginal costs** include future increases of capacity. The costs of these capacity increases have to be added to short-run marginal infrastructure costs.

- **Total and external costs**: Total costs are equal to the total amount of cost related to a period. External costs stand for that part of cost, which is not paid by the individual users. **External infrastructure costs** are equal to the difference between total infrastructure costs and the related revenues[5] (transport related taxes and charges). The difference is usually paid by the public. **External congestion costs** are equal to those costs which one vehicle imposes to the others being involved in congestion. Although that cost is paid by the users in total, they are external from the point of view of the individual road user. Since they are paid by the total of road users, they are internal from the point of view of the total road transport system. Consequently, they are relevant for determining optimal use of the network, but not for issues of cost recovery from road users.

---

[5]   As long as revenues are lower than costs.

Figure 1 summarises these definitions and the differences between the costs and expenditure categories explained above.

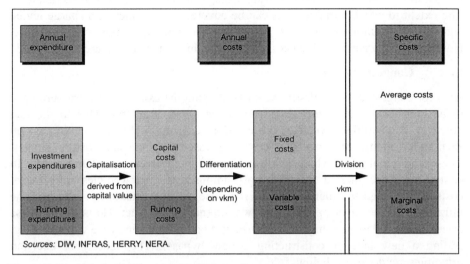

Figure 1: Interrelation between expenditure and cost categories

3.1.2   The interrelation between infrastructure and congestion costs: principles of efficient pricing

The interlinkage of infrastructure and congestion costs is important in order to explain the basic rules for infrastructure pricing[6] and to clarify the different purposes of road cost accounts concerning their methodological consequences. Therefore, it has to be distinguished between a state of no congestion (e.g. on rural roads) and a state of potential congestion (e.g. on an innerurban road link or on a bottleneck at motorways).

a)   Not congested roads

On these roads only those costs which arise from operating the existing infrastructure are relevant. This means that regarding the specific costs per vehicle-km, we have to discuss average costs and short-run marginal costs. Given the fact that the road is built, parts of the running costs (for example winter maintenance) do occur independently of additional vehicles. Thus, they are to be treated as fixed costs. Infrastructure investment costs are sunk costs. Marginal infrastructure costs (caused by additional vehicles) correspond to those costs

---

6   Note that we abstract in this chapter from further external cost components such as costs for accidents, noise, air pollution or climate change.

which depend on the use of roads (for example road pavement, additional maintenance). If owners or operators of the infrastructure intend to charge additional vehicles in an efficient way, a charge equal to these marginal costs has to be imposed. With the revenues of this charge the variable costs can be financed. The extent to which variable costs can be covered by revenues of a charge levied equal to short-run marginal costs, depends on the type of the marginal cost curve. However, in any case the fixed costs of the existing road network are not covered.

b)   Congested roads

Also for congested roads, firstly the costs of using the existing infrastructure have to be considered. Here, the statements made above hold true. Due to the fact however, that additional vehicles cause serious capacity problems, they impose on each other additional congestion costs expressed as time and operating costs. These additional costs which vehicles impose themselves are internal costs. In contrast to these internal costs, the costs imposed to other vehicles are external costs and express the inefficiency of road use. In this situation of scarcity, the infrastructure owner or operator has two alternatives to react: He might increase prices[7] in order to earn higher revenues and/or he might increase capacity (e.g. adding a new lane or constructing a new bypass). The underlying decision principles are described below.

In the short-run (no capacity increase) the user charge should be equal to the short-run marginal infrastructure costs (see section a) plus an additional fee which is equal to the marginal external cost of congestion[8]. This guarantees that individual road users pay for the specific marginal costs they cause. As soon as the annual revenues of these charges exceed the marginal infrastructure costs for enlarging capacity, it is worthwhile for the infrastructure operator to increase road capacity, since the additional cost for new investment is lower than the existing congestion cost. Thus, the existing congestion cost expresses the willingness to pay of users for additional road capacity. Figure 2 illustrates this interlinkage. While an optimal charge for an uncongested road is equal to marginal infrastructure cost, the charge for a congested road is equal to the sum of marginal infrastructure cost and marginal congestion cost. The revenues of this charge are equal to the integral of the difference between these two cost curves. If they exceed the investment costs for capacity increase, such investments are appropriate from the economic viewpoint. In that case the marginal infrastructure cost curve will be shifted up for a while. However, as soon as the new

---

[7] The additional individual time costs express the additional willingness to pay for using the road at a certain time.

[8] Due to the fact that usually a significant number of vehicles are involved in congestion and that it is complicated to consider the mutual effects, we neglect individual internal congestion costs. That means - as a simplification - external congestion costs are equal to total congestion costs.

infrastructure is constructed, marginal cost will decrease until the infrastructure is overutilised again and congestion with the respective costs would arise.

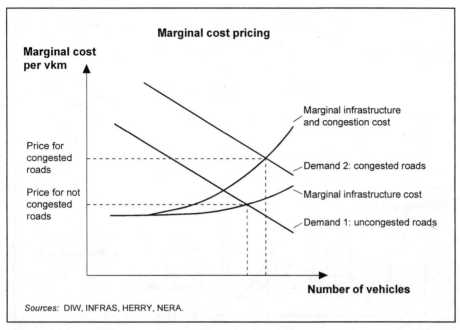

Figure 2: Interrelation between road infrastructure cost and congestion cost: marginal cost pricing

In practice (especially for electricity pricing and rail track pricing), more simplified schemes for infrastructure pricing are used in order to avoid these fluctuations. In privately operated businesses (in the road sector this concerns privately provided infrastructure), the operators are rather able to estimate the future costs of enlarging existing capacity than to estimate congestion costs. This fact leads to other practices in optimal infrastructure pricing which are illustrated in figure 3. The short-run fluctuations of marginal costs shown in the lower part of figure 3 can be avoided by charging an average price equal to the long-run marginal cost curve. This approach is called long-run marginal infrastructure cost pricing (Turvey and Anderson 1977).

It should be noted that both for using marginal congestion costs as a basis for pricing or for applying long-run marginal infrastructure cost pricing, the allocation rule is the same: As soon as the annual revenues of the charge exceed the annual cost of future infrastructure, it is worthwile to enlarge infrastructure capacity. Therefore, charging a price which reflects the welfare optimum in advance would require two types of information depending on the type of approach: While the information concerning the congestion cost required for congestion pricing is an information about the negative effect (the 'damage') of a bottleneck, the long-run infrastructure cost approach provides information about the avoidance costs of a bottleneck.

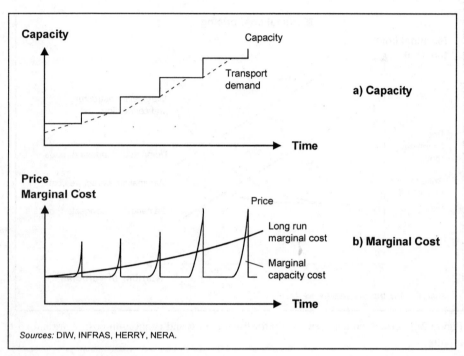

Figure 3: Interrelation between road infrastructure cost and capacity increase: long-run infrastructure cost pricing

3.1.3 External accident and environmental costs

So far we have treated infrastructure costs and congestion costs. However, road users usually cause other effects as well, which are known as external costs. These are:

– External costs of accidents, which are not covered by accident insurance and third party indemnity insurance,

– External environmental costs like damages on human health and buildings from air pollution, noise, increase of global warming risks, disturbance of landscape and severance etc.

These costs are not treated in this study. Since the estimation of these costs is rather difficult and their leverage points and pricing principles do not interfere directly with the principles of infrastructure pricing mentioned above, we can regard these costs as additional external costs causing further welfare losses.

3.1.4 Purposes of infrastructure cost calculations and methodological consequences

In general, three different aims for infrastructure cost calculations can be distinguished:

- Optimal pricing and efficient infrastructure allocation: The road users should face optimal price signals in order to guarantee an efficient use of existing infrastructure capacities and an efficient increase of capacity. This aim was treated in the previous chapters.

- Cost coverage: The users should bear the costs of road resources in order to preserve the economic value of the road network.

- Financing: The users should bear the financial burdens of road construction and road use in order to provide the annual financial means.

These three aims have different implications for the methodology to be used for cost estimation and, consequently, on the values of costs to be allocated to different types of vehicles (see table 4).

Since in practice each of these different aims should be achieved, they are mostly mixed up. As we have seen in the country review, in some countries capital cost accounts are used to compare annual revenues with the annual costs. In contrast to expenditure accounts, cost figures reflect the economic opportunity costs of existing infrastructure. Furthermore, the annual fluctuations are much lower. Therefore, cost accounts give more suitable implications for appropriate levels of taxation in the longer run. However, expenditure accounts are much easier to elaborate, because any capitalisation methodology and any long time series are not necessary.

Up to now, no country has developed a coherent calculation scheme based on marginal costs, which could serve as a direct basis for optimal pricing signals. Two arguments might be relevant for this situation: Firstly, the calculation of marginal costs (short-run marginal infrastructure and congestion costs, costs of infrastructure increase) is rather complicated. Secondly, the existing pricing principles are usually not very detailed (for example regarding vehicle types and user groups). Thus, they do not require differentiated cost figures, but are rather aimed at political acceptance and low implementation cost.

Table 4: Methodological implications of different aims of cost calculation

Aims of infrastructure accounts	Optimal pricing	Cost coverage	Financing
Relevance of type of cost	Marginal costs are relevant (short-run marginal costs and congestion costs). Fixed cost are sunk costs. They are thus not important for an optimal allocation of traffic.	Average cost are relevant (capital costs and running costs).	Annual financial burden is relevant, reflected by total annual expenditures.
Treatment of investments	New investments are long-run marginal costs. They have to be compared with marginal congestion costs in order to derive optimal enlargement paths.	Investments in the present and in the past have to be capitalized.	Annual investments are considered as annual expenditures. Capitalisation is not necessary.
Treatment of running cost	As long as they are variable costs, they form part of the short-run marginal cost.	Running costs are part of the average cost (not capitalized).	Running costs are part of annual expenditures.
Interrelation to congestion costs	Congestion costs can be interpreted as the costs of scarce capacity.	Indirect interrelation (Additional capital costs due to capacity increase). It is not sensible to integrate congestion costs into calculations of cost coverage.	Indirect interrelation (Additional expenditures due to capacity increase) It is sensible to integrate congestion costs into annual expenditure coverage.
Infrastructure accounts carried out for the respective aims yield mainly:	Short-run marginal costs per vkm as an indicator for non capacity pricing. Short-run marginal costs plus congestion costs as an indicator for capacity pricing.	Comparison of costs and revenues as an indicator for the cost coverage of different types of vehicle.	Comparison of annual expenditures and revenues as an indicator for the necessity of additional financial means.
Sources: DIW, INFRAS, HERRY, NERA.			

Within the context of fair and efficient pricing, infrastructure cost calculations have to serve as a basis for optimal pricing on the one hand and for a fair allocation of costs to users on the other hand. Thus, we can derive the following principles:

- Short-run efficiency on uncongested roads:

  → Marginal infrastructure costs

  The users have to pay at least for the marginal infrastructure costs. Thus, the infrastructure cost account has to elaborate these infrastructure costs directly. These costs should also be differentiated for the various types of vehicles, especially for HGVs. This implies, that the cost allocation method should enable these vehicle-type specific calculations.

- Efficient capacity management and enlargement:

  → Marginal congestion costs

  Scarcity prices have to be levied on roads with capacity problems and arising congestion costs. The optimal prices can be derived from existing marginal congestion costs. Optimal enlargement paths can be defined by comparing the revenues of congestion pricing and enlargement costs. However, it is not sensible to charge HGVs for their marginal congestion costs unless cars and other vehicles are treated in the same way, e.g. also have to pay for these costs.

- Fair allocation of fixed costs:

  → Average fixed infrastructure costs

  The users should pay their share of fixed cost. This aim can be achieved by calculating average infrastructure costs which are based on capital costs and running costs and which thus contain also the fixed costs. In order to avoid double counting pricing should take account of the fact that parts of the variable costs are already paid within a short-run marginal cost pricing.

Infrastructure cost accounts have to serve as a calculation basis for all these three elements. As far as infrastructure costs are concerned it is primarily the principles of short-run efficiency and fair allocation of fixed costs which are of importance. The calculation of marginal congestion costs however is especially necessary with regard to optimal capacity pricing. Due to the fact that congestion costs are related to all road users and thus have other implications than operator's infrastructure costs, the coverage of total congestion costs is not price relevant. Therefore, the calculation of total congestion costs is not the appropriate basis for pricing.[9]

Facing these principles it can be seen that purely financing aims are covered indirectly. Financing is not a principal goal of efficient infrastructure provision and traffic allocation. This implies that infrastructure accounts have to deal with

---

[9]   However, it might be useful to estimate total average congestion costs and compare them with other average cost figures (see chapter 3.6).

costs instead of expenditures. Annual expenditures are a basis to derive capital costs, but they do not reflect the value and the development of road resources in a proper way. To cover purely financial aims, specific expenditure flow charts may be used as a possible source of information.

3.2 Definitions and classifications

3.2.1 Expenditure types

The typisation of expenditures is of particular importance for the elaboration of cost based infrastructure accounts since the investive parts of road expenditures form the empirical basis for deriving capital costs. Thus, the following expenditure types for roads have to be distinguished within road cost accounts:

1. Investments

    They comprise net investments (construction of new roads, enlargement) and replacement investments.

2. Running expenditure

    This expenditure type contains

    – road maintenance,

    – road operation,

    – administration/police.

It is important to hint at the problem of how expenditures for replacement investments and maintenance expenditures are defined and delimitated. This distinction is realised in different ways in the European countries. Moreover, in most cases it is not transparent how these categories are delimitated. For example, Germany and Switzerland capitalise parts of maintenance expenditures. Germany defines - in line with the rules of SNA (Systems of National Accounts) - all maintenance measures with a life-expectancy of more than one year as replacement investments. For the future a common and transparent definition is necessary in order to achieve a minimum comparability of the data which the countries have to report to the Commission according to the EC-regulation 1108/70.

3.2.2 Treatment of value added tax (VAT)

Infrastructure cost accounts should represent the use of resources in a proper way. Thus, general taxes such as VAT should not be included. This is true both for the estimation of costs and of revenues, because revenues from general taxes such as VAT are not specific burdens of road users. Therefore, the existing national road accounts withdraw VAT from expenditure and cost figures.

This general rule, however, depends on the organisational status of road operation and construction. Operators of privatised roads (especially motorways in some EU countries) are on the one hand faced with construction costs etc. containing VAT. On the other hand, they owe VAT for their business to the government. For their pricing schemes, VAT has to be considered on the cost side. It is not clear whether and to what extent the tolls include VAT too. This issue has to be examined for each operator separately.

3.2.3 Definition of road infrastructure and road types

We define road infrastructure as all infrastructure which is required for motorised traffic including traffic safety areas and noise protection elements. This includes also space at the side of the road which can be used for parking.

In order to decide on the road types to be considered in our study, issues of definition/delimitation and classification of roads in the EC-countries are important. As far as definition issues are concerned, mainly the question arises whether forest roads should be included. We decided to exclude forest roads.[10] Regarding road classification two main streams in the European countries can be distinguished:

Classification I:

> I a) interurban roads

> I b) urban roads

Classification II:

> II a) high classified roads:

> – motorways

> – expressways

> II b) medium classified roads:

> – trunk roads

> – provincial roads

---

10 The exclusion of forest roads was discussed with the Steering Committee of the project. Especially the representatives from Austria and Sweden voted for including these roads because of their relatively high share in the total road length. Finally, it was decided to exclude forest roads because of the insufficient data situation.

II c) low classified roads:

- district roads (for example so-called Kreisstraßen in Germany)
- municipal roads

Road cost accounts should be based on a common classification of roads in Europe. Given the fact that mileage and expenditure data for most road types are lacking, we propose to elaborate road cost accounts for the total road network excluding forest roads. We will consider motorways separately if the data situation allows this. For some countries only cost calculations for the national road network (mostly comprising motorways and trunk roads) are possible due to the lack of data for the remaining road categories.

3.2.4 Vehicle categories

The vehicle types considered in existing cost or expenditure accounts vary from country to country. The differences concern mainly the number of weight classes and axle configurations considered, the definition of weight classes themselves[11] and the question whether trailers are treated separately. Furthermore, there are also differences in the national definition of a vehicle category.

We propose to consider in our cost calculations the following vehicle set:

- rigid goods vehicles (lorries without trailer with a permitted max. GVW ≥ 3.5 t);

- lorries with trailer (including ordinary tractors with trailer, except agricultural vehicles);

- articulated vehicles (tractors with semi-trailer).

However, one should bear in mind that in particular agricultural vehicles and special vehicles also contribute to road deterioration.

---

[11]   For example, in Germany exists in the category of rigid good vehicles a class from 9 t up to 12 t max. GVW. In Switzerland this class ranges from 7.5 t up to 15 t max. GVW.

3.3 Estimation of capital values and capital costs

3.3.1 Capital values

Estimating the value of capital stocks in industrial sectors is a common procedure within the Systems of National Accounts (SNA) in most OECD-countries. However, more detailed estimates of capital values than for industrial sectors - for example for infrastructure assets like roads, railways, waterways, airports etc. - are lacking in most countries. According to the rules of SNA, the capital value for these infrastructure assets is in most countries included in the figures for the sector transport and telecommunications. Apart from the problem that these values are not separately elaborated and published, it has to be borne in mind that the SNA determines not to depreciate public construction investments for infrastructure. Thus, in the official results of SNA for these assets the gross value is considered to be equal to the net value and any information on the level of depreciation (one important cost component) does not exist.

Estimates for road capital values within Europe are presently only available for Germany, Austria, Denmark, Finland, Sweden and Switzerland. Road capital values and annual capital charges for the trunk road network in the UK are currently being prepared, but have not yet been published.

Table 5 gives an overview on the different approaches applied in six European countries for estimating road capital values. As can be seen from there, the capital values for roads can be estimated by two approaches:

1. Synthetic method (direct evaluation of assets)

Within the synthetic method the assets are directly evaluated based on an inventory of the road system. The main principle is described in section 3.3.1.1. This method requires comprehensive information on network characteristics for different road sections in order to determine the asset's value of these sections. The synthetic method is used in Austria and Finland. Some countries (e.g. Denmark) use this method to create initial values as a starting point for the indirect method.

2. Indirect method by modelling approaches (perpetual inventory concept)

Due to the huge expense of labour and time the synthetic method is usually not applied within the SNA. Most OECD-countries use the perpetual inventory method, often based on an initial value obtained by applying the synthetic method. The perpetual inventory concept which is described in section 3.3.1.2 capitalises time series of annual investment expenditures. This concept requires detailed and long time series on annual investment expenditures, information on life expectancies of assets, and initial values. Within Europe, the perpetual inventory concept is applied for the estimation of road capital values in Germany, Finland, Denmark, Sweden and Switzerland.

Apart from the two approaches mentioned above, private motorway companies (for example in France, Italy, Portugal and Spain) present figures for the capital value of their companies within the annual balance sheets. However, these values are not comparable with those derived with the other two methods since they are elaborated as entrepreneurial figures based on other evaluation principles, depreciation periods etc. The road capital values for countries with private motorways require thorough analysis and comparison with the values derived with the other methods. This analysis, however, was not up to this study.[12]

3.3.1.1 The direct (synthetic) method

The synthetic method has been used if

- the data (long investment time series) for the perpetual inventory concept are not available,

- the perpetual inventory concept is for other reasons not applicable (for instance for methodological reasons), or

- the initial values for applying the perpetual inventory concept in future studies have to be elaborated.

With the synthetic method the asset types are directly evaluated by estimating the costs which would occur if it were intended to replace the whole road network with assets of equivalent quality. Thus, the existing physical assets have to be measured in terms of indicators such as length, width, number of lanes, tunnels, bridges etc. and to be evaluated by unit replacement costs. This approach requires to define asset groups which are depreciation-relevant, homogeneous and practicable regarding the availability of unit replacement costs.

---

[12]   Therefore, table 5 excludes capital values for privately owned roads.

Table 5: Methodological concepts for estimating road capital value and capital costs[1]

Methodological issue	Austria	Denmark	Finland	Germany	Sweden	Switzerland
Estimation of capital values/ Type of capital value	synthetic method (direct evaluation of assets) gross value	perpetual inventory concept (based on expenditure time series from 1950 onwards) net value	detailed inventory of all assets of public roads net value	perpetual inventory concept (based on expenditure time series from 1856 onwards) both gross and net value	perpetual inventory concept net value	perpetual inventory concept (based on expenditure time series from 1919 onwards) net value
Evaluation of capital costs	replacement costs (obtained with the annuity method)	purchase costs	replacement costs	at constant prices	at constant prices	purchase costs
Asset types	detailed distinction between different - infrastructure groups - road types - road sections	corresponding with expenditure categories	4 asset types: – earthwork/ tracking/ drainage – pavement – bridges/tunnels – equipment	4 asset types: - earthwork - bridges/tunnels - pavement - equipment	roads as a homogenous asset considered	corresponding with expenditure categories: – new investments and improvement – investive main-tenance
Life expectancies	Land : infinite Tracking/Layers: 90 years pavement: 45 years surfacing: 15 years tunnels: 90 years Bridges: 75 years	40 years for total road capital	Land: infinite Earthwork/tracking/ drainage: 50 years pavement 10 years bridges/tunnels: 85 years equipment: 10 years	calculated by probalistic functions for asset types within defined intervalls: Land: infinite earthwork: 1-180 years bridges/tunnels: 5-110 years pavement: 5-55 years equipment: 1-30 years	land: infinite others: 40 years	land: infinite new inv./ upgrading: 40 years investive maintenance: 12,5 years
Depreciation method	within the annuity method	linear	linear	linear	linear	linear
Interest rates	real interest rate for public loans: 3%	nominal interest rate: 8.7% (1994)	up to now no interests calculated, for further studies planned	real interest rate for public loans: 2.5%	none[2]	nominal interest rate (floating average) for public loans 1994: 5.3%
Evaluation of land costs	land purchase cost (no depreciation)	land purchase cost (no depreciation)	land purchase cost (no depreciation)	land purchase cost (no depreciation)	land costs are not considered within the capital value	land purchase cost (no depreciation)

[1] Excluding private road infrastructure (such as in France, Italy, Portugal and Spain) for which capital values are not calculated with the aim of estimating capital costs, therefore any interest rate is not applied. - [2] In Sweden road capital values are derived from entrepreneurial accounting principles.

Source: Review of studies and national statistics, carried out by DIW, INFRAS, HERRY, NERA.

3.3.1.2 *The indirect method - perpetual inventory concept*

General description

The main idea behind the perpetual inventory concept is to calculate the asset's value by cumulating the annual investments and by subtracting either the value of those assets which exceeded their life-expectancy (written down or „lost" assets) or the depreciations. This principle is expressed in the equations below:

$$VG_{t+1} = VG_t + I_{t,t+1} - A_{t,t+1} \qquad\qquad (1)$$

$$VN_{t+1} = VN_t + I_{t,t+1} - D_{t,t+1} \qquad\qquad (2)$$

with: VG_t :   Gross value of assets at time t

   VN_t :   Net value of assets at time t

   $I_{t,t+1}$:   Investments during t, t+1

   $A_{t,t+1}$:   „Lost" assets during t, t+1 (assets which exceeded life-expectancy)

   $D_{t,t+1}$:   Depreciation during t, t+1

As shown in these formulas the perpetual inventory method can be applied for estimating the **gross value** (gross concept) and the **net value** (net concept) of road assets. The gross value contains the value of all assets which still exist physically in the considered year, e.g. which have not yet exceeded their life expectancy. Thus, $A_{t,t+1}$ means those assets which could not be used any longer or which were shut down. It is assumed that the assets are properly maintained and can be used until they exceed their defined life-expectancy. Within the net-concept the annual depreciations $D_{t,t+1}$ are considered. The net value of assets describes the time-value of all assets which have not yet exceeded life-expectancy. According to the international conventions of the SNA, most countries use a linear depreciation method. Figure 4 demonstrates the main principle of the perpetual inventory concept for a single asset.

The use of the perpetual inventory concept requires detailed time series of investment expenditures in order to consider technically homogeneous investment types with the respective life-expectancies. Depending on the asset's type these time series have to reach very long back into the past. Furthermore, an initial value for the capital stock is required except the case that the available investment time series exceeds the life expectancy of assets. The advantage of the perpetual inventory concept lies - compared with the synthetic method - in the possibility to continue these calculations annually in a relatively easy way with a lower expense of labour and time, provided the basic work of building up the model is done and an initial value exists.

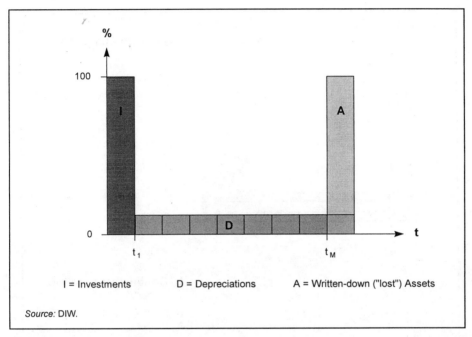

Figure 4: Interrelation between investment, written-down („lost") assets and depreciation - the case of a single asset

Refined perpetual inventory models with survival functions

As can be seen from table 5 there are four countries which apply the perpetual inventory concept for the estimation of road capital values. Out of these, Germany and Sweden use rather refined perpetual inventory models. In contrast to perpetual inventory models applied in other countries it is assumed that the life-expectancies of assets within an investment-vintage are dispersed on the mean value. On this basis a probability function, the so-called survival-function, was estimated which describes the share of assets which are still in use. The inverse function which describes the „lost" assets $A_{t,t+1}$ was estimated as a polynom of third degree in Germany (see figure 6). Sweden uses a survival curve of the Winfrey-type (see Tengblad 1993).

The use of probability functions implies that not single assets but technically homogeneous groups of assets (earthworks, bridges/tunnels, pavement and equipment) are considered. For these asset groups long investment time series have to be available.[13]

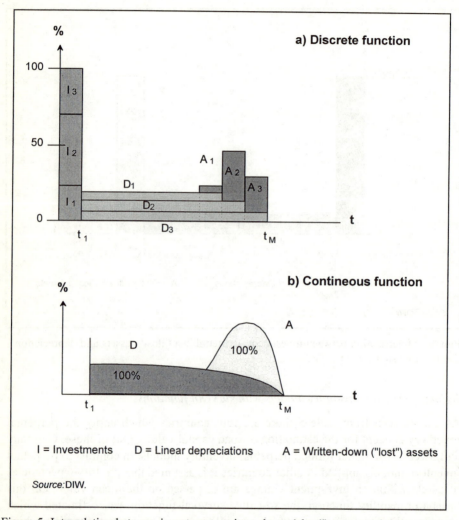

Figure 5: Interrelation between investment, written-down („lost") assets and depreciation - the case of an asset group

---

[13]   However, there are considerable differences in the differentiation of asset types and in the assumptions on life expectancies of roads in Germany and Sweden. The German model contains four asset types with different life expectancies (116 years for earthworks, 35 years for pavement, 68 years for bridges and tunnels) while in Sweden roads are considered to be a homogeneous asset with an average service life of 40 years.

The difference between the more simplified approach of considering single assets and the more refined approach with asset groups is shown in figure 4 and figure 5. Figure 4 illustrates the interrelation between investment, physical „loss" of the asset and depreciation for a single asset while figure 5 demonstrates the inter-relation between these categories for an asset group (for example pavement). The approach shown in figure 5 considers the fact that the investment spent for an asset group consists of parts with different life expectancies which are dispersed within an interval around the mean. Although for example also in the German method for all elements of the investment I_1 - I_n a linear depreciation is applied, the overall asset group shows in fact a degressive depreciation due to the underlying type of probability function for the „lost" assets (as shown in the lower part of figure 5).

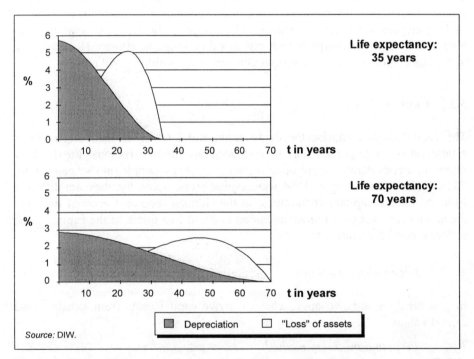

Figure 6: Shape of the curve for the „lost" assets and the depreciations as applied in Germany - for different life expectancies -

3.3.1.3 Capital values in entrepreneurial accounts

We already hinted at the fact that private motorway companies derive the capital values from entrepreneurial principles, considering taxation rules etc. Such capital values and the corresponding capital costs are thus not comparable with figures compiled rather under macro-economic aspects for publicly financed infrastructure. The main differences concern:

- other depreciation periods,
- other depreciation methods,
- other evaluation principles for the gross fixed capital formation (profit expectations),
- other methods for calculating capital values (for companies usually by inventories, for national assets mostly with the perpetual inventory method).

In our study this problem occurs for Portugal, Italy and France. However, it should be noted that this is not only a problem for road capital values. It arises also when infrastructure cost accounts for railways shall be elaborated and public rail companies are to be compared with privatised ones. If one intends to compare such entrepreneurial capital values with those elaborated by applying the perpetual inventory concept, the net capital value should be chosen. However, due to the issues mentioned above serious comparability problems will remain.

3.3.2   Capital costs

The capital costs comprise the depreciation and interest of road assets. Their estimation is an important part of cost accounts for two reasons: Firstly, they represent a considerable share of total road costs. For example, in Germany about 70 % of total road costs in 1994 were capital costs. Secondly, they are different from the annual capital expenditures. In the German road cost account for 1994 the annual capital expenditures amounted to about two thirds of the capital costs; in Switzerland the share was 72 %.

3.3.2.1 Depreciation methods

In general there are two approaches to derive capital costs from existing road capital values.

1.   Perpetual inventory method

The depreciation is calculated within the perpetual inventory concept usually by applying a linear depreciation method. For the remaining value of assets interests are calculated (concerning the calculation of interests see chapter 3.3.2.2).

2.   Annuity method

Within the annuity method depreciation and interests are contained in an annuity which is calculated according to the known annuity formula:

$$a = u \cdot \frac{\dfrac{z}{100} \cdot \left(1 + \dfrac{z}{100}\right)^{d}}{\left(1 + \dfrac{z}{100}\right)^{d} - 1} \tag{3}$$

with: a   -   annuity for the capital value

u   -   capital value

z   -   interest rate in percent

d   -   depreciation period (years) for the road assets.

This formula gives the annual amount for refinancing road investments. The advantage of the first method is that a distinction between depreciation and interest can be made, which gives transparency on the value of these cost components. However, since it is based on the perpetual inventory method, the same comprehensive data base is necessary which is not available for many countries. The advantage of the annuity method is the easy application which does not require any long investment time series. However, a differentiation between the level of depreciation and interest cannot be made.

3.3.2.2 Interest

In this section we discuss which interest rates are most appropriate to calculate capital costs. In this discussion mainly three aspects have to be considered:

- Interest rates on which capital?

Within the relevant literature (for example DIW 1987, Aberle and Holocher 1984) two opinions do occur:

In one point of view, it is necessary to derive capital costs for the whole road capital. This includes interest, since they reflect the opportunity cost of the road capital (i.e. the potential gains from investing the money in other sectors).

Another point of view extends the discussion to the revenue side and argues, that interest rates are only to be considered for that amount of road capital which is not financed by the revenues collected from the users. This opinion has a virtual enterprise in mind which invests money in the road sector and yields money from the users (although the different taxes and charges are in reality not (fully) earmarked). Thus, interest is calculated from annual deficits of this virtual enterprise.

In order to derive the full economic costs, we do not consider this second approach as an appropriate one. It does not reflect economic reality and it is not applicable since the calculation of interests should be based on all previous periods as well.

- Private or public capital costs?

The interest rate has to reflect the opportunity costs of capital invested in the road sector. Since roads are mostly financed with public money, an interest rate reflecting the costs of public capital is appropriate. Usually, there do not exist any direct loans for financing the construction of roads. Thus, the interest rate on ordinary government loans should be used. However, these interest rates are not stable in time. In order to avoid the annual fluctuations, it would be appropriate to calculate an average of all running governmental loans (weighted with their respective payment periods). If this information is not available, the actual interest rate can be applied.

- Nominal or real interest rates?

We have stated above that capital values should be derived with the perpetual inventory method which uses replacement costs (i.e. constant prices which consider the annual inflation rate). This has implications for the choice of the appropriate interest rate. Nominal interest rates contain the inflation premium, whereas real interest rates do not. This means: The use of the replacement cost approach requires the application of a real interest rate, whereas the purchase cost method has to consider a nominal interest rate. Since the replacement cost method uses a specific (road infrastructure related) inflation rate, this method is much more precise than the purchase cost method with a nominal interest rate, because the sector-specific inflation rate is already considered within the capital values.

3.3.3 Discussion of the methodological differences

The capital values estimated with different methods in European countries are the basis for calculating capital costs. Therefore, it is important to clarify to what extent methodological differences influence the level of capital values and capital costs. In order to make these impacts transparent, the methodological issues listed above and their consequences have to be discussed and quantified:

- consequences of the general approach chosen for estimating capital values (synthetic method versus perpetual inventory concept),[14]

---

[14]   Since the problems of comparing entrepreneurial capital values (as available for private motorway companies) with capital values calculated rather from the macro-economic viewpoint were already discussed in paragraph 3.3.1.3 we mention here only the problems within the macro-economic approaches.

- simplified perpetual inventory models (Switzerland, Denmark) versus more refined ones with survival functions (Sweden, Germany),

- consequences of the assumptions and parameters set in the approaches: life expectancies (all countries), type of survival function (Sweden/Germany),

- consequences of evaluating capital values at purchase costs or at constant prices,

- calculating capital costs within the perpetual inventory concept or with the annuity method.

In this study, not all of these issues can be discussed in a quantitative manner. For example, a comparison of the results yielded with the synthetic method on the one hand and with the perpetual inventory concept on the other hand is not possible because there is no country for which results of both approaches are available.

Impacts of model types and parameters

Figure 7 and figure 8 demonstrate the impacts of different modelling approaches (simple and refined perpetual inventory model) and different life expectancies on the capital costs. The results were derived from road investment time series for Switzerland and for West Germany.[15] As can be seen from there a generalised statement (such as: „Higher life expectancies lead to higher capital costs") cannot be concluded. Moreover, the figures show clearly that there are different effects. These effects result for example from:

- the shape of the investment time series,

- the model chosen,

- the life expectancy assumed, and

- the interest rate applied.

The combination of these factors influence both the level and the structure of capital costs. It should be noted that in the results of our sensitivity analysis the characteristics of „real world" investment time series are mixed up with impacts of modelling approaches, parameters etc. More detailed analyses with simulated different types of time series would be required for separating these effects.

---

[15]   For these countries long investment time series, required for this sensitivity analysis, are available.

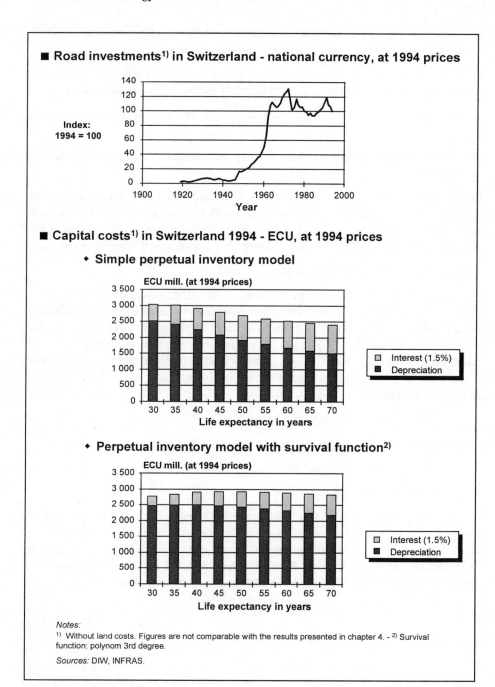

Figure 7: Capital costs calculated for different life expectancies with two modelling approaches - Swiss data

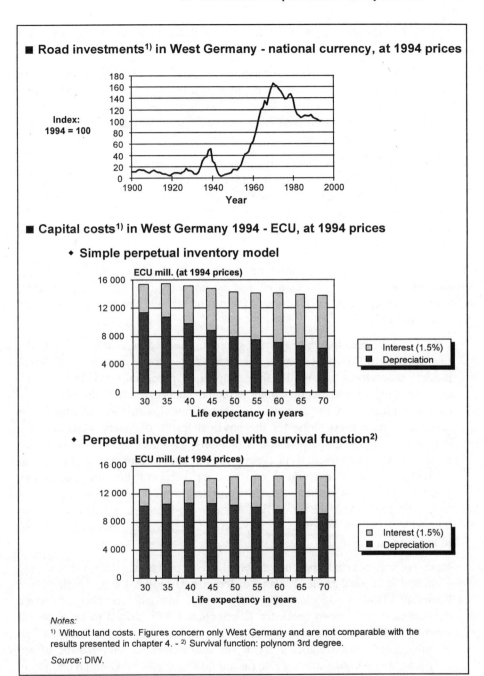

Figure 8: Capital costs calculated for different life expectancies with two modelling approaches - West German data

Analysing the results presented in figure 7 and figure 8 we can observe the following:

- Both for Swiss and for West German data an increase of lifetime leads in the simplified perpetual inventory model to a clear reduction of capital costs. This overall reduction of capital costs is exclusively caused by decreasing depreciations while the interest costs increase (since the interest rate is applied to a higher net capital value).

- In the more refined perpetual inventory model an increase of life expectancy leads (up to a life expectancy of 45 to 50 years) to higher capital costs. Assuming life expectancies of more than 50 years we can observe a slight fall (Swiss data) and stagnation (German data) respectively. Apart from this, the share of depreciations in the total capital costs is higher than in the simple perpetual inventory model.

As already stated, an explanation of these results has to consider both the characteristics of the time series used and the impacts of models and parameters which occur independent on the type of input time series. Here we can summarise the following effects:

1. First, it can be seen that the capital costs are influenced in different ways in the two models, if life expectancies are increased. This is caused by different model characteristics. While the simplified perpetual inventory model calculates the annual depreciations as equal sums over the life expectancy (linear depreciation), the perpetual inventory model with survival functions[16] assumes a right-skew slope for the physical losses of assets which gives a degressive fall for the depreciations (actually the curve has an S-shape, see figure 6). This implies that, in contrast to the simple model, the majority of depreciations are concentrated on the first years of the life expectancy intervall. This leads on the one hand to another development of capital costs in time (compared with the simplified model). On the other hand, it results in higher depreciation (absolute values) and in a higher share of this component in total capital costs.

2. Next, we can see that applying different life expectancies within the refined perpetual inventory model leads to different cost curves for Switzerland and Germany. This is explained by the level of interest rate charged. Since decreasing depreciations (both for Germany and Switzerland to be observed from 45 and 50 years onwards) raise the net capital value, the interest rate can be interpreted as a weighting factor (or multiplier) for this growth of net capital value. A higher interest rate (as applied for the West German data) may consequently outweigh decreasing depreciations.

---

[16]   Here applied as a polynom of 3rd degree.

Impacts of evaluating capital costs (nominal versus real terms)

Table 6 compares the capital costs derived by evaluating the investments at purchase costs and applying a nominal interest rate with those capital costs yielded by using a real interest rate and calculating the capital value out of investments at constant prices. Due to availability of data, this sensitivity analysis was carried out for Switzerland only. While the two approaches do not lead to any significant differences for the motorways, the capital values for the total road network differ by more than 10 %. As stated in chapter 3.3.2.2 it is more precise to calculate capital costs by evaluating the investments at constant prices and applying a real interest rate because this method distinguishes between a sector-specific and an average inflation rate.

Table 6: Sensitivity analysis for calculations of capital costs in real and nominal terms for Switzerland 1994 and 1995

Capital Costs[1)][2)]	Offical calculation (at current prices)		Alternative calculation (at constant prices)[3)]	
	CHF mill.	ECU mill.	CHF mill.	ECU mill.
1994				
Total road network	4 620	2 850	5 240	3 230
Motorways	2 480	1 530	2 480	1 530
1995				
Total road network	4 770	3 080	5 280	3 420
Motorways	2 600	1 680	2 550	1 650

[1)] Including land costs. Calculated as average over the year. - [2)] Only costs of road use for transport related functions. - [3)] At 1994 and 1995 prices.

Sources: BFS 1997, INFRAS.

Perpetual inventory approach versus calculating annuities

Table 7 contains the capital costs obtained with the annuity method and the respective results with the perpetual inventory concept, both applied for German data. As can be seen from table 7 the annuity method underestimates the capital costs compared with the results from the more sophisticated perpetual inventory model. The range of underestimation reaches from one third to one quarter which is a not negligible level. Similar results were yielded for Switzerland where the capital costs for 1994, calculated with the annuity method, amounted to only 60% of those calculated with the perpetual inventory method. The reason for these differences is that within the annuity method the capital charges are calculated without any information about the age structure while the perpetual inventory concept takes into account the age composition of the capital stock.

Table 7: Comparison of capital costs calculated with two methods for Germany[1]

Year of cost account	Annuity Method Capital costs in DM mill.	Perpetual Inventory Method Capital costs in DM mill.	Annuity Method in % of Perpetual Inventory Method
1978	11 560	14 900	77.6
1981	16 260	21 200	76.7
1984	17 490	21 800	80.2
1987	19 440	24 270	80.1
1991	24 480	30 400	80.5
1994	25 270	37 330	67.7

[1] 1978, 1981, 1984, 1987, 1991 West Germany, 1994 Germany. Depreciation periods: earthworks: 116 years, bridges/tunnels: 70 years, pavement: 33 years, equipment: 18 years; real interest rate: 2.5 % p.a.

Source: DIW.

3.3.4 Consequences for the methodology proposed for this study

As the explanations of concepts in this chapter showed, we can distinguish three groups of countries in regard to the estimation of capital values and capital costs.

Group 1: Countries which apply the perpetual inventory method. To these countries belong Germany and Sweden (both with a more refined version of the perpetual inventory method), Switzerland, and Denmark.

Group 2: Countries which apply the direct (synthetic) method. These are Austria, France, Finland and Denmark (estimation of the initial value).

Group 3: Countries for which no estimates on road capital values do exist.

First of all, we propose to apply for the countries of the first and the second group the method already used, without harmonisation of model structures. We consider this as appropriate since the refinement of these methods would require a much better data base and a huge expense of labour and time.

Secondly, we have to decide on a method to be applied for those countries which do not have any estimates of road capital values up to now. For these countries we propose two approaches: For countries like the UK, Ireland, Belgium, the Netherlands and Spain, which have longer investment time series (at least for 30 years) we apply a simplified perpetual inventory method. This implies that depreciation is also calculated within the perpetual inventory model.

For countries without any sufficiently long investment time series only rough estimates on the basis of indicators like km-values in comparable countries are possible. If more appropriate and thoroughly elaborated capital values are to be derived these countries need to carry out a direct evaluation of road capital stocks (as done in Denmark and Finland) which could then easily be updated by applying the perpetual inventory method. For these countries we suggest calculating capital costs with the annuity method which, however, at least requires information on depreciation periods (life expectancies). However, one has to be aware of the underestimation of costs with this approach. Nevertheless, we consider this as a practicable way. It seems not to be sensible to apply sophisticated depreciation methods to capital values which are only roughly estimated.

3.4 Cost allocation

Cost allocation is a breakdown of global costs to lower levels which can be

- road functions (transport functions and non-transport related functions as well as non-motorised transport, as described in section 3.4.1),
- road types (road specific cost allocation),
- vehicle types (vehicle specific cost allocation described in section 3.4.2),
- domestic and foreign vehicles (origin specific cost allocation).

In this study we will concentrate on the allocation of costs to vehicle types. Furthermore, we discuss briefly how to treat non-motorised transport and non-transport related functions.

3.4.1 Non-transport related functions

Before allocating road infrastructure cost to different types of motorised vehicles, it has to be considered that not all infrastructure is exclusively used by motorised traffic. Roads are also constructed and used for other purposes, such as:

- Non-motorised transport like pedestrians and bicycles
- Market space and access function
- Infrastructure synergies (e.g. canalisation)

The discussion of non-transport related functions is on the one hand linked with the delimitation of the road network (see above). On the other hand, it is related to the discussion on external benefits of road infrastructure as for example separation benefits (fire walls) and on option values for other uses (e.g. military).

We think that these functions have to be considered within the elaboration of road cost accounts. Thus, it is necessary to define a share of road costs, which has not to be charged to motorised traffic. This share differs between the types of road. In order to determine the extent of non-transport related functions, we can distinguish two principles:

- Users view: The share of non-transport functions can be derived from the intensity of road use by non-motorised users.

- Causation view: The share depends on the historical reasons to build and to enlarge a certain road.

Reviewing the practice in different European countries, there is only limited empirical evidence. Usually the separation of non-transport functions is rather pragmatic. Only three countries apply explicit factors:

- Germany: Implicit interest reduction for urban roads. In total the share is about 6%.

- Austria: Explicit assumptions on shares for motorways (0-10%), trunk roads (20-30%) and implicit shares for communal roads (>20%).

- Switzerland: Explicit assumptions on shares for motorways (0%), trunk roads (10%) and communal roads (30%).

These assumptions are mainly based on rough estimations of road use for non-motorised purposes and non-traffic related functions.

3.4.2   Approaches for cost allocation to vehicle types

In principle there exist two types of allocation procedures for breaking down global costs to vehicle types:

- Deterministic procedures which are characterised by a more or less arbitrary definition and allocation of cost components.

- Procedures which quantify functional relationships between vehicle specific costs and traffic performance figures (such as vehicle-km, gross-weight-km, standard-axles*vkm, PCU-km and vehicle-length* vkm).

For allocating infrastructure costs to vehicle types the costs have to be categorised. In that context, the most important distinction between cost categories is those between fixed and variable costs:

1.   Fixed costs are independent of the traffic volume. In literature they are sometimes also to be found under the term capacity cost. Because of this

independency, any direct allocation of these costs to vehicles is not possible. Nevertheless, they depend on the expected volume of traffic (e.g. the dimension of a newly constructed road). Thus, the allocation methods practically used consider the extent to which the different types of vehicles use the road capacity. Usually vkm, speed-dependent and length-dependent equivalence factors are applied to allocate these costs.

2. Variable costs depend directly on the use of the road. Out of these costs, a very important component is the weight dependent part (for example for road maintenance like surface dressing etc.). Therefore, the allocation method for these cost categories is very sensitive to HGV related parts. A widely used allocation rule are the results of the AASH(T)O road test carried out by the U.S. Highway Administration. [17]

Reviewing the practice in different countries of Europe, it can be stated that although the principles are similar, the approaches are quite different: This concerns within the **deterministic method** (for example applied in Denmark, Germany and Switzerland) the traffic performance variables used (vehicle-km, gross weight-km etc.). They are defined exogenously, based on specific studies and vary from country to country. The equivalent factors applied for the allocation of capacity costs relate to passenger cars (PCU's = passenger car units) but are based on different criteria such as capacity, speed and space required by vehicles. For instance the German capacity cost allocation is based on speed-dependent equivalent factors (see table 8) while in Switzerland vehicle-length dependent allocation factors and simply the mileages driven are used (see table 11). For allocating weight-dependent cost components it is common to use the AASH(T)O-factors based on the results of the AASH(T)O-test.

In contrast to the countries mentioned above, only Austria uses the **statistical cost allocation method.** The reason why other countries base their cost allocation method on the deterministic approach might be found in the higher expense of time and labour and the comprehensive data requirements. It should also be mentioned that the final results of the Austrian allocation procedures are a combination of the statistical cost allocation method and the German allocation method which belongs to the deterministic approaches.

In the following we analyse the more sophisticated methods applied in different countries.

Austria

The Austrian cost allocation procedure combines three methods:

- Method 1: full statistical method

---

[17] See for example: Highway Research Board: The AASHO-Road Test - History and Description of Project. Special Report 61 A. Washington D.C. 1961.

- Method 2: partly statistical method

- Method 3: DIW method.

For applying the methods 1 and 2 to Austrian data, functional equations were estimated by a multi-linear regression system for motorways, expressways and trunk roads. For each of these road types the total costs were differentiated into current costs and (capitalised) investment costs. Various traffic performance data (vehicle-km, GVW-km, length-vehicle-km, duration of road usage and standard-axle-km) were taken into account. The shares a_v of the total costs allocated to vehicle types result then from the following (matrice-) equation:

$$
\begin{pmatrix} a_1^{ik} \\ \dots \\ a_v^{ik} \\ \dots \\ a_{22}^{ik} \end{pmatrix} = \begin{pmatrix} p_{11}^{ik} \cdots p_{1j}^{ik} \cdots p_{15}^{ik} \\ \dots \\ p_{v1}^{ik} \cdots p_{vj}^{ik} \cdots p_{v5}^{ik} \\ \dots \\ p_{221}^{ik} \; p_{22j}^{ik} \cdots p_{225}^{ik} \end{pmatrix} * \begin{pmatrix} \bar{p}_1^{ik} \\ \dots \\ \bar{p}_j^{ik} \\ \dots \\ \bar{p}_5^{ik} \end{pmatrix}
$$

(4)

with:

p_{vj} regression coefficient of vehicle category v and traffic performance variable j

$\bar{p}$ regression coefficient concerning traffic performance variable j

i type of road (motorway, expressway or trunk road), $i = 1,2,3$

k type of cost (capital or running cost), $k = 1,2$

j type of traffic performance variable (vehicle-km, ...), $j = 1, ... ,5$

v type of vehicle category, $v = 1, ..., 22$.

If the coefficients $\bar{p}$ are obtained from a regression model too, the method is called a full statistical method (method 1). If these values are estimated directly from the performance figures a partly statistical method is applied (method 2). Both methods were used in Austria. Additionally, the German method (see the description for Germany below in this chapter) was applied. In order to yield more consistent HGV-shares a weighted average of these three methods was calculated.

Germany

The German cost allocation belongs to the non-statistical methods. It distinguishes between **marginal** costs and **capacity** costs (= total costs minus marginal costs). The basic assumption of the German cost account is that the total cost curve is characterised by a linear shape. Hence, the marginal costs are constant and equal to the variable costs per unit output. In the German cost accounts the costs of police, the costs of pavement maintenance and the costs of pavement replacement are considered as marginal costs. In the first German infrastructure cost study for 1966 regression analyses for these cost categories were carried out and later on for some sample years updated. These analyses showed that the share of marginal costs in the total road costs is low.

Table 8: The German cost allocation procedure

Costs	Cost category	Cost allocation per traffic performance variable	
		Equivalent-factor-km	Standard-axle-weight
Marginal costs	Costs of police	0.0 %[1]	0.0 %[1]
	Costs of pavement maintenance	0.0 %	100.0 %
	Costs of pavement replacement	0.0 %	100.0 %
Capacity costs		100.0 %	0.0 %
[1] Costs of police are allocated by vehicle-km. *Sources:* BMV, DIW.			

The traffic performance variables used for the German cost allocation are:

- Equivalent-factor-km (using the speed-dependent equivalent factors given in table 8) for allocating capacity costs. The equivalent factors take account of the fact that the road capacity is to a different extent occupied by the vehicle types. The basic idea behind the equivalent factors used in the German cost accounts is that these occupancy differences are based on different speeds and not on the occupied space. Within the basic study in the late 60s, the different speeds of vehicles mainly on gradient sections of the road network were investigated. The equivalent factors were derived from these investigations by considering the share of gradient sections on the total road network.

- AASHO-factor-km (using the AASHO-factors shown in table 9) for allocating marginal costs (except the costs of police which are allocated by vehicle-km).

Table 9: Equivalence factors[1] for capacity cost allocation in Germany

Vehicle Categories	Equivalence Factors
Bicycles	0.33
Mopeds, bicycles with engine, light motorcycles	0.33
Motorcycles	0.50
Passenger cars	1.00
Agricultural vehicles	6.00
Ordinary tractors with trailer	6.00
Lorries	
< 3.5 t GVW	1.70
3.5 t - 9 t GVW	2.20
9 t - 12 t GVW	2.70
12 t - 18 t GVW	4.30
> 18 t GVW	5.80
Ordinary trailer	3.00
Articulated vehicles	6.00
Other vehicles[2]	6.00
Coaches/buses	3.00
Trams	8.00

[1] Speed-dependent factors for considering the vehicle-specific occupation of roads. - [2] Special vehicles, agricultural vehicles.

Sources: BMV, DIW.

Table 10: AASHO-factors used in the German cost allocation procedure

Lorries, Special vehicles		Buses		Trailers		Articulated Vehicles	
Weight classes (max. GVW/ axle configurations)	AASHO-factor	Weight classes (max. GVW/ axle configurations)	AASHO-factor	Weight classes (max. GVW/ axle configurations)	AASHO-factor	Weight classes (max. GVW/ axle configurations)	AASHO-factor
2 axles		2 axles		2 axles		2 + 1 axles	
< 2 t	0.0001	< 2 t	0.0001				
2 t - 3 t	0.0014	2 t - 3 t	0.0002	< 3 t	0.0004		
3 t - 3.5 t	0.0029	3 t - 3.5 t	0.0005	3 t - 3.5 t	0.0005		
3.5 t - 4 t	0.0031	3.5 t - 4 t	0.0011	3.5 t - 4 t	0.0015		
4 t - 5 t	0.0048	4 t - 5 t	0.0023	4 t - 5 t	0.0026		
5 t - 6 t	0.0089	5 t - 6 t	0.0030	5 t - 6 t	0.0044		
6 t - 7 t	0.0197	6 t - 7 t	0.0101	6 t - 7 t	0.0061	< 6 t	0.0026
7 t - 7.5 t	0.0217	7 t - 7.5 t	0.0157	7 t - 7.5 t	0.0122	6 t - 7 t	0.0046
7.5 t - 8 t	0.0287	7.5 t - 8 t	0.0230	7.5 t - 8 t	0.0177	7 t - 9 t	0.0095
8 t - 9 t	0.0470	8 t - 9 t	0.0294	8 t - 9 t	0.0299	9 t - 10 t	0.0142
9 t - 10 t	0.0716	9 t - 10 t	0.0459	9 t - 10 t	0.0483	10 t - 12 t	0.0296
10 t - 12 t	0.1167	10 t - 12 t	0.0825	10 t - 12 t	0.0906	12 t - 14 t	0.0429
12 t - 14 t	0.3547	12 t - 14 t	0.1609	12 t - 14 t	0.1969	14 t - 16 t	0.0793
14 t - 16 t	0.6351	14 t - 16 t	0.2852	14 t - 16 t	0.3808	16 t - 18 t	0.1559
16 t - 17 t	1.1509	>16 t	0.5000	16 t - 17 t	0.4121	18 t - 20 t	0.2750
17 t - 18 t	1.6500			17 t - 18 t	0.7970	20 t - 24 t	0.3316
18 t - 19 t	2.2000						
3 axles		3 axles		3 axles		2+2 axles	
3.5 t - 9 t	0.0070					18 t - 20 t	0.1451
9 t - 14 t	0.0600			10 t - 12 t	0.0279	20 t - 24 t	0.2932
14 t - 16 t	0.3006	14 t - 16 t	0.1052	12 t - 14 t	0.0600	24 t - 28 t	0.4864
16 t - 18 t	0.5512	16 t - 17 t	0.1539	14 t - 16 t	0.0907	28 t - 32 t	1.1711
		17 t - 18 t	0.1948	16 t - 17 t	0.1349	32 t - 34 t	1.2424
18 t - 20 t	0.5800	18 t - 19 t	0.2434	17 t - 18 t	0.2566	34 t - 36 t	2.0741
19 t - 20 t	0.5968	19 t - 20 t	0.3005	18 t - 19 t	0.2813	36 t - 38 t	2.5138
20 t - 22 t	0.6681	20 t - 22 t	0.4039	19 t - 20 t	0.3460	3+2 axles	
		22 t - 24 t	0.5812	20 t - 22 t	0.4629	28 t - 32 t	0.7435
		24 t - 26 t	0.8117	22 t - 24 t	0.4828	32 t - 34 t	1.1001
				24 t - 26 t	0.6800	34 t - 36 t	1.2538
				26 t - 28 t	1.0000	36 t - 38 t	1.7085
						> 38 t	2.6135

Source: BMV, DIW.

Switzerland

In the Swiss cost allocation method the total costs are divided into running costs, weight dependent costs and capacity costs (= total costs minus running costs minus weight dependent costs).

The traffic performance variables used for the cost allocation are vehicle-km, vehicle-length-km, axle-weight-factor-km and standard-axle-weight-factor-km. The axle-weight-factors and the standard-axle-weight-factors were derived from the AASHO-road test but reduced to the 2,5th power of the axle-weight-factors (instead of 4th power). Table 11 shows the main issues concerning the Swiss cost allocation procedure.

Table 11: The Swiss cost allocation procedure

Costs	Cost category	Cost allocation per vehicle category	Cost allocation per road type	Cost allocation per traffic performance variable			
				Vehicle-km	Vehicle-length-km	Axle-weight-factor-km	Standard-axle-weight-factor-km
Weight dependent costs	Costs for new investment	HGV	Motorways: 5.6 % of the costs for new investments	0.0 %	0.0 %	100.0 %	0.0 %
			Principal roads: 5.5 % of the costs for new investments	0.0 %	0.0 %	100.0 %	0.0 %
			Communal roads: 4.2 % of the costs for new investments	0.0 %	0.0 %	100.0 %	0.0 %
	Costs for investive maintenance	HGV	45 % of the costs for investive maintenance for all roads	0.0 %	0.0 %	0.0 %	100.0 %
Running costs		All vehicles	All roads	100.0 %	0.0 %	0.0 %	0.0 %
Capacity costs		All vehicles	All roads	20.0 %	80.0 %	0.0 %	0.0 %
Sources: BFS, INFRAS.							

United Kingdom

Although for the UK any cost-based road account does not exist, a sophisticated allocation method for road expenditures is applied. Total expenditures are divided into current expenditures, capital expenditures and expenditures for policing and traffic wardens. These cost items are differentiated for motorways, trunk roads, principal roads and other roads. The traffic performance variables used for the UK expenditure allocation are vehicle-km, average-gross-vehicle-weight-km, maximum-gross-vehicle-weight-km, standard-axle-weight-factor-km and passenger-car-unit-km (PCU-km). Table 12 summarises the UK expenditure allocation procedure while table 13 shows the parameter values of average-gross-vehicle-weight, standard-axle-weight and passenger-car-unit.

Table 12: The UK expenditure allocation procedure

Expenditure item	Percentage of costs of item allocated to:					
	Vehicle-km	Maximum-GVW-km	Average-GVW-km	Standard-axle-weight-km	PCU-km	Pedes-trians[1]
	in %					
Capital expenditure	-	15	-	-	85	-
Maintenance expenditure						
1 Reconstruction and resurfacing	-	-	-	100	-	-
2 Haunching	-	-	100	-	-	-
3 Surface dressing and skid treatments	20	-	80	-	-	-
4 Patching and minor repairs	-	-	20	80	-	-
5 Drainage	100	-	-	-	-	-
6 Bridges and remedial earthwork	-	-	100	-	-	-
7 Grass and hedge cutting	100	-	-	-	-	-
8 Sweeping and cleaning	50	-	-	-	-	50
9 Traffic signs and pedestrian crossings	100	-	-	-	-	-
10 Road marking	10	-	90	-	-	-
11 Footways, cycle tracks and kerbs	-	-	50	-	-	50
12 Fences and barriers	33	-	67	-	-	-
13 Winter maintenance and miscellaneous	100	-	-	-	-	-
14 Street lighting	50	-	-	-	-	50
Police and traffic warden	100	-	-	-	-	-

[1] Except on motorways, where no allocation is made to pedestrians and all expenditure is allocated to vehicles.
Source: DETR.

Table 13: Parameter values of average-gross-vehicle-weight, standard-axle-weight and passenger-car-unit in the UK expenditure allocation procedure

Vehicle class	Parameter values		
	Average GVW	Standard axle	PCU
Cars, light vans and taxis[1]	1.0	0.00002	1.0
Motorcycles	0.1	0	0.5
Buses and coaches	8.7	0.16	1.5
Goods vehicles over 3.5t GVW	4.3 - 26.3	0.008 - 0.911	2.0
Other vehicles[2]	2.3	0.007	1.4

[1] Includes goods vehicles under 3.5 tonnes GVW. – [2] Crown, disabled and other vehicles exempt from VED, haulage, machines, 3-wheeled motor vehicles, special types, recovery vehicles and non-plateable vehicles.
Source: DETR.

Denmark

The Danish road cost account distinguishes between administration costs, winter maintenance costs, other maintenance costs, reconstruction costs and capital costs. These items are differentiated for motorways, trunk roads, principal roads and communal roads. The traffic performance variables used for the Danish cost allocation are vehicle-km, vehicle-length-km and standard-axle-weight-factor-km. Table 14 summarises the Danish cost allocation procedure.

Table 14: The Danish cost allocation procedure

		Fixed costs	Variable costs			
			Vehicle-km	Vehicle-length-km	Standard-axle weight-km	Total
		in %	in %	in %	in %	in %
Administration	Motorways and trunk roads	70	30	0	0	100
	Principal and communal roads	80	20	0	0	100
Winter maintenance	Motorways and trunk roads	50	30	20	0	100
	Principal and communal roads	50	30	20	0	100
Other maintenance	Motorways and trunk roads	70	20	10	0	100
	Principal and communal roads	70	20	10	0	100
Reconstruction	Motorways and trunk roads	30	0	25	45	100
	Principal and communal roads	50	0	10	40	100
Investment	Motorways and trunk roads	0	45	40	15	100
	Principal and communal roads	0	80	15	5	100

Source: COWI.

Finland

In the Finnish expenditure allocation method the maintenance costs are further differentiated into winter maintenance, maintenance of paved roads, maintenance of light-paved roads, maintenance of gravel roads, traffic guidance and information, landscaping and sanitation, bridges, ferries etc. Furthermore, also capital expenditures are allocated. These expenditure types are available for public roads (state owned roads) and streets (road owned by municipalities). The traffic performance variables used for the Finnish expenditure allocation are vehicle-km and load-equivalence-factor-km. The load-equivalence-factors are presented in table 15, the allocation of maintenance expenditures is detailed in table 16.

Table 15: Load-equivalence-factors in the Finnish expenditure allocation procedure

Vehicle type		Allocation factor
Lorries	3.5 t - 18 t	0.18
	18 t - 26 t	0.87
	26 t - 44 t	1.2
	44 t - 53 t	2.56
	53 t - 60 t	2.97
	more than 60 t	4.6
passenger cars and vans		0.0003
Source: LT Consultants.		

Table 16: Allocation of maintenance expenditures in Finland

	Fixed expenditures in %	Variable expenditures allocated		Total in %
		per vkm in %	per weight in %	
Winter maintenance	95	5	0	100
Maintenance of paved roads	25	50	25	100
Maintenance of light-paved roads	25	25	50	100
Maintenance of gravel roads	40	25	35	100
Traffic guidance and information	70	30	0	100
Landscaping and sanitation	100	0	0	100
Bridges	50	25	25	100
Ferries etc.	75	20	5	100
Source: LT Consultants.				

The Netherlands

A commonly accepted and applied method for cost allocation to vehicle type does not exist in the Netherlands. In DHV/Tebodin 1992 one method is described and applied for 1990 data, however, only for a small set of vehicle types. This method is based on an earlier infrastructure expenditure study carried out in 1981.

Table 17: The Dutch allocation procedure

	Investment expenditures			Maintenance/Operation/Overhead expenditures			
	capacity costs 85 %	weight dependent costs 10 %	others 5 %	fixed costs	variable costs		
	allocated by vkm * PCU[1]	allocated by vkm * axle-load 4th power	treated as maintenance/overhead expenditures allocated by the respective allocation factors (see categories I - IV)	allocated by vkm *PCU[1]	allocated by vkm* PCU[1]	allocated by vkm * axle-load 1st power	allocated by vkm * axle-load 4th power
				category I 42 %	category II 29,6 %	category III 11,5 %	category IV 16,9 %
				– maintenance of bridges, tunnels, retaining walls – maintenance of earthwalls – grass and hedge cutting – traffic signs, traffic surveillance, telephones – street lighting – drainage – maintenance of bicycle lanes and sidewalks	– winter maintenance (snow sweeping, sand) – street marking – safety measures	– treatment of road surface (thin tar/ asphalt layers) – partial maintenance measures for pavements – repair of road holes, etc.	– pavement renewal – other reconstruction measures

1) As PCU's are used: passenger car = 1, rigid goods vehicles = 2, goods vehicle combinations = 3. Source: Dienstweg- en Waterbowkunde en TU Delft.

Source: DHV/Tebodin 1992.

In this allocation method the total expenditures are divided into investment expenditures on the one hand and four categories of maintenance/operation/overhead expenditures on the other hand. The traffic performance variables used for expenditure allocation are PCU-km, axle-load 1st power-km and axle-load 4th power-km. Details of this allocation procedure can be taken from table 17.

Sweden

The Swedish cost allocation method was developed in DsK (1987:11) and updated in Hansson (1996). It distinguishes between investment expenditures and maintenance/other expenditures which are both differentiated for federal roads and municipal roads. All expenditure items are subdivided into fixed and variable costs. Within these two groups the allocation factors used are vehicle-km, PCU-km and ASSHO-factor-km. Table 18 contains the main issues of the method.

Table 18: The Swedish cost allocation procedure

Cost items	Fixed costs % allocated by			Variable costs % allocated by	
	vkm	vkm * PCU	vkm * AASHO-factors	vkm	vkm * AASHO-factors
Investments					
- Federal roads		79	21		
- Municipal roads		74	26		
- Private roads		92	8		
Increase in bearing capacity			100		
Maintenance/Operation expenditures					
Federal roads					
- Winter road maintenance	95				5
- Paving maintenance	25				75
- Bridges	67			13	20
- Ferries & bridge oper.	75			20	5
- Gravel road maintenance	40			25	35
- Driving supervision, etc.	90			10	
- Traffic security	90		10		
- Improvement measures	75		25		
- Municipal roads					
- Paving maintenance	20			40	40
- Winter road maintenance	95				5
- Bridges, etc.	60			20	20
- Other	100				10
Private roads	74		6	10	

Source: Hansson (1996) based on „Costs of Heavy Road Traffic" (DsK 1987:11) with some modifications.

3.4.3 Discussion of the differences of the approaches

The previous chapter showed that there is a considerable variety of cost allocation methods used by the countries investigated. Therefore, the essential differences and the respective consequences of the approaches have to be analysed. A quantitative comparison of different cost alloction methods has never been done in Europe before. Thus, this part of our study is particularly important since it provides for the first time quantitative knowledge on the sensitivity of methods when applied to different data-sets.

We conducted sensitivity analyses of the most important European methods with available data sets. The allocation methods used in cost/expenditure studies in Germany, Switzerland, Sweden, the Netherlands, UK and Denmark were applied to data from Austria, Germany and Switzerland.[18]

Table 19 gives an overview of the results and figure 9 visualises the overall results.

Table 19: Application of different cost allocation methods to Austrian, German and Swiss data

Results for	Vehicle category	Method-type applied						
		D	DK	UK	CH	A	NL	S
		Share of costs allocated to vehicle types in %						
Austrian data	Passenger cars / Buses[1]	57.2	86.5	79.5	82.7	57.2	82.2	67.9
	Trucks	19.9	3.9	6.7	6.7	18.4	9.4	7.3
	Articulated vehicles	22.9	9.6	13.8	10.6	24.4	8.4	24.8
	Total	100.0	100.0	100.0	100.0	100.0	100.0	100.0
German data	Passenger cars / Buses[1]	53.2	67.8	52.1	81.7		72.4	59.5
	Trucks	23.6	9.4	38.0	8.1		15.0	18.3
	Trailer	8.0	12.2	2.9	4.2		2.9	6.5
	Articulated vehicles	7.9	6.1	4.7	3.8		5.7	10.4
	Others[2]	7.3	4.5	2.3	2.2		4.0	5.3
	Total	100.0	100.0	100.0	100.0	n.a.[3]	100.0	100.0
Swiss data	Passenger cars / Buses[1]	72.1	80.3	80.0	87.0		81.4	63.9
	Trucks	22.0	10.5	11.5	9.8		13.6	29.6
	Trailer	2.6	4.7	3.5	1.4		2.2	1.9
	Articulated vehicles	3.5	4.5	6	1.1		2.8	4.6
	Total	100.0	100.0	100.0	100.0	n.a.[3]	100.0	100.0

[1] Including light goods vehicles (vehicles with a max. GVW < 3.5 t) and motorcycles/mopeds. - [2] Special vehicles, ordinary tractors with trailer, and agricultural vehicles. - [3] The Austrian method requires comprehensive regression analysis and was not applicable due to lacking data.
Sources: DIW, INFRAS, HERRY, NERA.

---

[18]   In these countries genuine and detailed cost accounts exist and the data base is sufficient to apply the allocation methods mentioned above.

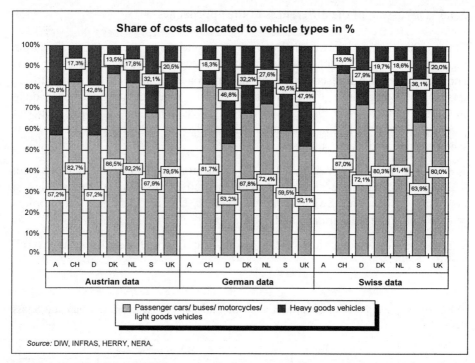

Figure 9: Application of different cost allocation methods to Austrian, German and Swiss data

As can be seen from table 19, using different methods for a certain set of data leads to a quite significant range of results. The cost share of HGV yielded by applying the different allocation methods varies

- for Austrian data from 13.5 % to 42.8 %

- for German data from 18.3 % to 47.9 %

- for Swiss data from 13% to 36.1%.

However, the ranking of the different methods concerning the share of costs allocated to HGV is not the same in the three countries investigated. For example, it is not in all cases the same allocation method which yields for the three data sets the highest share of costs allocated to HGV. An overall interpretation of the results has to consider the following aspects:

- The methods applied have various effects. The extent to which the cost categories are differentiated and allocated by different factors varies among the allocation methods. One of the most important issues is the share of costs which are allocated by weight-dependent allocation factors. This share differs considerably among the allocation methods as table 20 points out for the German data set.

- The weight-dependent allocation factors differ regarding their differentiation for vehicle categories, weight classes and axle configuration. While for example the AASHO-factors are available in very detailed differentiation (applied in the German, Austrian and Swiss allocation method), there exist only five weight dependent allocation factors for goods vehicles in the Danish method. Furthermore, we can observe differences concerning their values (e.g. reduced AASHO-factors in the Swiss method). The same holds true for the length- and speed-dependent factors.

- The traffic situation in the countries investigated have different characteristics. To be mentioned are aspects like topography, network characteristics (e.g. tunnels, bridges) and HGV shares. This is especially true for Switzerland with a mountainous area and a 28 ton max. GVW limit. Therefore, differences in the results of one method applied for different countries (e.g. application of the German method to German, Swiss and Austrian data) reflect reality.

- The interpretation and transferability of the various cost categories within the applied methods cause quite significant problems. One example of this data differentiation, which is a necessary precondition to apply the methods, is the distinction between new investments, improvement, replacement investments and investive parts of maintenance. Sensitivity analysis has shown that the assumptions for these categories (especially for weight dependent costs) are quite sensitive.

Table 20: Shares of cost allocated by different factors within the investigated methods, applied to German data

Applied allocation method	Share of weight-dependent cost allocated by standard axles or other weight factors	Gross weight/ average weight	Share of vkm and length/speed dependent cost
D	16%		84 %
DK	20%		80%
UK	37%	10 %	53%
CH	3%		97%
NL	9%		91%
S	25%		75%
Sources: DIW, INFRAS, HERRY, NERA.			

It is difficult to separate the effects of these aspects. Further research with qualitatively improved data would be necessary. Nevertheless, some basic conclusions can be drawn which are important in order to define a harmonised method.

- For all countries, the German method leads to a remarkably high cost share of HGV. The reason for this lies in the progressive effect of applying the AASHO-factors. Furthermore, the German method reacts quite sensitive concerning the estimation of the share of marginal cost. Analysis has made clear that the empirical basis for estimating these shares is weak.

- The Swiss method leads to rather HGV friendly cost shares. This is mainly caused by the low share of costs allocated by weight dependent factors. Thus, it can be stated, that this method is a 'Swiss speciality' mainly applicable for Swiss road characteristics and traffic conditions (28 tonne limit).

- The UK method allocates a high share of costs by weight-dependent factors. Thus, it is very sensitive, if one has to transfer the respective cost categories to the UK-classifications. This is one reason why for instance Germany yields a quite high HGV share with this method, while in Switzerland, this share is rather low. Furthermore, the fact that the UK-method uses a number of different allocation procedures for the various cost categories limits the transferability of this method to other than UK-data.

- The Swedish allocation procedure belongs to the methods which allocate a comparable high share of costs to HGVs. With the distinction between fixed and variable costs for each item of expenditures it can be characterised as a transparent method. Furthermore, it provides sound preconditions in order to derive marginal costs. However, the necessary very detailed categorisation of expenditures for different road types complicates transferability.

- The Danish allocation method leads to rather moderate shares of HGV cost. The results lie mostly between those obtained with other methods. The transferability is rather easy. However, the estimation of the weight related factors is not very transparent.

- The Dutch allocation method yields results similar to those obtained with the Danish method. Like the Danish method it is rather easy to transfer to country-specific data.

3.4.4 Consequences for a harmonised approach

The analysis in the previous sections has shown that at this stage of research and given the availability and quality of data, not all effects of the allocation methods used in Europe can be explained. Thus, the choice of one method as „best" method or the creation of a generalised cost allocation method for all EU-countries seems not to be sensible. For the empirical work in chapter 4 the following approach will be used:

- Total road infrastructure costs have to be divided into the following categories:

- Fixed cost (Cost shares of capital and running cost): considered as capacity cost.

- Variable cost.

• It seems appropriate and practicable to use three cost allocation factors for these cost categories:

  - Capacity costs have to be allocated according to vkm and equivalent factors. The basis for the equivalent factors has to be defined (speed-/length-dependent) and may vary from country to country.

  - Variable costs should be allocated by standard axles and vkm.

• For those countries which already apply an own method of cost allocation, their method is defined as the basic calculation. Other methods might be used for sensitivity analysis in order to interpret the results properly.

• For the other countries, the use of allocation factors should be transparent and allow for considering countrywise features/specialities. Given the methodological differences described in the previous sections, it is necessary to be flexible in choosing weight dependent cost shares.

3.5 Estimation of marginal infrastructure costs

As stated in chapter 3.1 it is short-run marginal costs which are important for pricing under the aim of efficient use of existing infrastructure. Up to now, no country has elaborated a method for estimating marginal costs. Some empirical studies calculate marginal infrastructure costs either by defining marginal costs as variable costs or by using more or less arbitrary defined shares of the variable costs. However, as pointed out in section 3.1 variable costs are per definition not equal to the marginal costs. Estimating marginal costs would actually require to know the total cost function or at least to have information on the shape of the total cost curve. Additionally, the problem arises that the chosen time horizon has impacts on the definition/delimitation of marginal costs (e.g. short-run versus long-run marginal costs). For example, the design of a new road clearly depends on the type and volume of traffic expected on this road. The construction costs related to the expected traffic situation (gradients, radius of curves, thickness of layers, etc.) are to some extent to be considered as variable and consequently marginal costs.

In Germany there were attempts in the late sixties to derive marginal infrastructure costs for roads and railways by regression analysis between different cost categories and traffic performance. However, similar in-depth analysis has not been continued and the share of marginal costs in the total costs has simply been interpolated and adjusted to changed conditions (for example inclusion of East

Germany) in all successor studies. To our knowledge, there are not any similar in-depth studies on marginal costs in other EU-countries which could serve as a basis for our study.

Within the PETS-project[19] the costs of bridge maintenance and the costs of reconstruction and resurfacing are considered to be relevant for charging HGV on the basis of short-run marginal costs. Again however, it should be noted that these costs are variable costs but not necessarily to the full extent marginal costs. Additional problems occur for countries where maintenance expenditures are partly capitalised, as it is usual in Germany and Switzerland.

The time limit of our study did not allow to carry out basic regression analyses actually required for estimating marginal costs. We consider this as a very important task for future research. We choose a rather pragmatic approach to provide some first results on the level of marginal costs for roads in EU-countries. We consider - with variations from country to country - parts of maintenance expenditures (maintenance of bridges and tunnels, pavement, resurfacing) as marginal costs. Furthermore, also parts of reconstruction are to be considered as variable and thus also to some extent as marginal costs. These components were - for example for Germany - also included into the marginal costs. These basic principles are applied and adjusted to country-specific conditions (including data availability).

3.6 Congestion costs

In this section of the study we consider congestion costs, and particularly the relationship between goods vehicles and congestion. In doing this, it is necessary to distinguish between the congestion costs that goods vehicles **suffer**, because they are slowed down by other vehicles[20], and the congestion costs that they **cause**, by slowing down other vehicles.[22] It will also be very important to distinguish between the **average costs** of congestion and the **marginal costs** of congestion. It is the latter that is particularly important with regard to optimal pricing to make the most efficient use of the road network.

3.6.1 The definition of congestion and congestion costs

First, it is necessary to define more precisely what we mean by congestion. We can do this by noting that on any road network there will be travel times and travel

---

[19]   ITS et al.: Pricing European Transport Systems. Project for the EC-Commission within the Fourth Framework Programme Transport. In progress.

[20]   Including other goods vehicles.

costs which will be achieved by vehicles of particular types when traffic levels are "low". We refer to these traffic levels as the **reference** level. In practice actual travel times and operating costs might exceed times and costs with reference traffic levels because of the existence of higher volumes of traffic. In practice the definition of these "low" traffic levels (reference levels) is complicated and depends not only on the type and qualitative characterisation of road but also on the vehicle-structure of traffic flows. The definition of reference levels may vary from country to country: The American Highway Capacity Manual (HCM) (see HCM 1992) distinguishes six levels of service (LOS) while Germany used until the middle of 80es a three-levels concept.

We can define the total cost of congestion as the difference between the total costs of travel (including both money costs and time costs) of existing traffic flows, and the costs of travel if all this traffic could move at the costs and times which would be achievable on the network when traffic levels were "low".[21] We therefore do need to be able to define what we mean by "low" traffic levels and the associated traffic speeds that can be achieved with these low levels of traffic flow if we wish to measure the **total** level of congestion.

The average cost of congestion suffered by a particular type of vehicle is then equal to the difference between the money plus time cost which the vehicle actually incurs, and the money plus time costs of making the same journey with the reference traffic level.

On the other hand, the marginal cost of congestion is equal to the **extra** money plus time costs imposed **on all other vehicles** by the addition of an **extra** vehicle to a traffic flow. This is equal to the increase in journey cost and time to each vehicle in the traffic flow, added up over all vehicles in that flow. Marginal costs of congestion imposed by a single extra heavy goods vehicle will be greater than those imposed by an extra car, because a heavy goods vehicle takes up more road space than a car, and has different speed and acceleration characteristics. (Note that marginal costs of congestion depend on the actual volume of traffic, but **not** on the reference level of speed.)

3.6.2   The measurement of congestion costs

We next consider how average and marginal costs of congestion can be calculated in practice, using one particular approach. We should note, however, that all methods of calculating congestion costs will require us to value travel time in order for us to provide overall monetary values for congestion costs.

---

[21]   Other costs such as potential losses of third parties if goods are not delivered in time can be defined as indirect impacts of congestion. As long as there is a market between the operator and the shipper these costs are paid (for example expressed in conventional fines) and are thus internalized.

The approach to be considered uses two types of relationship:

1. Speed-flow curves, familiar to highway engineers, which show a mathematical relationship between traffic flows on a road (usually in terms of vehicles per lane per hour), and the resulting traffic speeds on that road; and

2. Operating cost formulae, which show a relationship - for a particular type of vehicle - between cost per km and speed. Since there is an exact inverse relationship between the speed and the time taken to travel one kilometer, time values can be incorporated into these formulae.

Combining these formulae gives a mathematical relationship between the volume of traffic flow on any section of road, and the cost of travel along that section of route. This means that it is possible to calculate both the average cost of congestion and the marginal cost of congestion for any traffic flow level.

To show how this can be made operational, we can demonstrate by reference to the approach adopted by NERA to look at British traffic congestion,[22] using the tools developed by the UK Department of the Environment, Transport and the Regions (henceforth DETR) to measure the benefits of new roads.

The DETR uses piecewise linear speed-flow curves, as illustrated in figure 10. The shape and position of this curve will depend on the type of road. The vertical intercept, v_f, can be defined as the "free-flow" speed, the speed which is obtained when there is only one vehicle per hour.[23] Each downward-sloping section of the speed-flow curves has an equation of the form:

$$v = A - B \cdot F \tag{5}$$

where v is the actual speed, F is the traffic flow in vehicles per lane per hour, and A and B are constants determined by the characteristics of the road, and by the particular segment of the "curve" which covers a range of traffic flows.

---

[22]   Dodgson, J.S. and Lane, B. (1997): The Cost of Road Congestion in Great Britain. NERA. London.

[23]   Some speed-flow curves have an initial horizontal segment, indicating that speeds initially do not fall as more vehicles join the traffic flow.

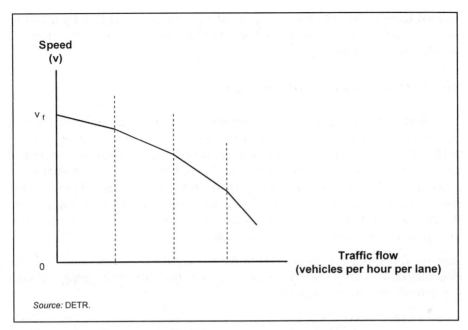

Figure 10: Speed-flow curve for the UK

The UK DETR use operating cost formulae of the form

$$g = a + b/v + c \cdot v^2 \tag{6}$$

where g is operating cost per kilometre for a particular type of vehicle, including time costs. The term g is therefore known as "generalised" cost, i.e. money plus time cost per km. As before, v is speed in km per hour, and the terms a, b and c are parameters which vary between different types of vehicle. The term b incorporates a part which equals the value of occupants' time per hour for that particular type of vehicle.

3.6.2.1   The average and total costs of congestion

The average cost of congestion per km is therefore equal to the difference in the value of g for that particular type of vehicle at the actual speed and the value of g for that particular type of vehicle evaluated at the reference (or "free flow") speed. The value of generalised cost at the actual speed might be calculated using data on actual speeds, or it might be evaluated by predicting the actual speed using data on actual traffic flows, combined with the relevant speed-flow curve.

NERA calculated this for Great Britain, and then aggregated over all vehicles to derive the total costs of congestion in 1996, using very detailed traffic flow data for 26 different types of road and nine time periods of the day or week. This enabled them to estimate the total costs of congestion suffered by rigid and by articulated heavy goods vehicles in 1996 in different parts of the road system and at different times of the day.

3.6.2.2   *The marginal costs of congestion*

To calculate the marginal cost of congestion, we need to combine the two mathematical functions from formulae (5) and (6) to derive a relationship between traffic flow and generalised cost per vehicle. We can then differentiate generalised cost with respect to traffic flow, and evaluate the value of this differential at the actual traffic flow. This shows the way in which an extra unit added to the traffic flow changes the generalised cost of travel for another vehicle in the traffic flow. We then need to sum all these changes over all other vehicles in the traffic flow. This gives us the marginal cost of congestion.

Suppose first of all that all vehicles in the traffic flow are of the same type, for example cars. Then, from formulae (5) and (6), the relationship between generalised costs and traffic flow is:

$$g = a + [\,b\,/\,(A - B \cdot F\,)\,] + c\,[\,A - B \cdot F\,]^2 \qquad\qquad (7)$$

and the marginal cost of congestion is:

$$(\partial g\,/\,\partial F) \cdot F = [\,b \cdot B\,(A - B \cdot F)^{-2} - 2 \cdot c \cdot B\,(A\text{-}B \cdot F)\,] \cdot F \qquad\qquad (8)$$

In words, the marginal cost of congestion can be calculated from data on the actual traffic flow (F), and the slope parameter (B) of the speed-flow relation[24], and the variable parameters (b and c) of the generalised cost formula.

Now suppose that the traffic flow consists of five types of vehicles:

1. cars;

2. light goods vehicles;

3. rigid heavy goods vehicles;

4. articulated goods vehicles; and

5. buses.

Now we have first to allow for the fact that these different vehicles make different contributions to congestion, e.g. an extra articulated goods vehicle slows down the average traffic speed more than does an extra car. This is usually allowed for by weighting vehicle numbers by passenger car units (pcus), where a car has a value

---

[24]   Where the speed-flow curve has a number of linear segments, the value of B will depend on the range within which the traffic flow value F lies.

of one, and other types of vehicles have values which reflect their relative contribution to congestion.

We now need to reinterpret the hourly traffic flow in terms of PCU-weighted vehicles, i.e.

$$F = F_1 + PCU_2 \cdot F_2 + PCU_3 \cdot F_3 + PCU_4 \cdot F_4 + PCU_5 \cdot F_5 \tag{9}$$

An extra car will then impose additional congestion costs on all other vehicles in the flow equal to:

$$(\partial g1/\partial F) \cdot F_1 + (\partial g2/\partial F) \cdot F_2 + (\partial g3/\partial F) \cdot F_3 + (\partial g4/\partial F) \cdot F_4 + (\partial g5/\partial F) \cdot F_5 \tag{10}$$

An extra articulated heavy goods vehicle (vehicle type 4) will impose extra congestion costs on the rest of the traffic flow equal to:

$$PCU_4 \left[(\partial g_1/\partial F) \cdot F_1 + (\partial g_2/\partial F) \cdot F_2 + (\partial g_3/\partial F) \cdot F_3 + (\partial g_4/\partial F) \cdot F_4 + (\partial g_5/\partial F) \cdot F_5 \right] \tag{11}$$

where PCU_4 is the number of cars equivalent to one extra articulated heavy goods vehicle.

Again the terms $\partial g/\partial F$ for each vehicle class can be measured from the speed-flow and generalised cost parameters, as was shown above in equation (8).

3.6.2.3 Data requirements

What would be needed to apply this approach to different countries? To apply this particular approach we need:

1. Traffic flow data per lane per hour in PCUs, split by type of vehicle if we wish to distinguish between marginal congestion costs caused by different types of vehicle;

2. Slopes of the speed-flow curves (or a non-linear mathematical function for the speed-flow curve) [25] ;

3. Vehicle operating cost parameters which incorporate values of time. The parameter a is not needed. In practice the value of c is very small (it represents the way in which fuel costs per km rise with very high speeds) and this part of the generalised cost equation can be dispensed with. The value of time will vary from country to country (though it should bear some relationship with average hourly earnings). The price of fuel per litre will vary from country to

---

[25] Dodgson (1986) calculates congestion costs in Australian cities using a non-linear speed-flow relationship. Dodgson, J.S. (1986): "Benefits of changes in urban public transport subsidies in Australia". Economic Record 224-235. Reprinted in Glaister, S. (1987): Transport Subsidy, Policy Journals, Newbury.

country, and data on these prices are readily available across countries[26]. Operating characteristics of particular types of vehicle will vary mainly because of differences of the composition of the fleet in different countries, e.g. small cars in Italy. However, the main differences in the generalised cost parameters will arise because of differences in time values, since time accounts for by far the largest proportion of the speed-dependent part of generalised costs.

3.6.3 The approach for congestion costs adopted in the present study

3.6.3.1 *The relevant concept of congestion*

Given that the Commission's Green Paper on transport pricing emphasises the importance of **securing efficiency** in the transport sector, and points out that this implies that charges should be related to short-run marginal costs to secure optimal use of existing infrastructure, we believe that the appropriate approach in the present study is to calculate marginal congestion costs. These costs are **external** to individual road users and hence do not influence their decision on whether or not to travel on congested roads. Consequently pricing is needed to ensure that road users do take these real costs into account when making their decisions.

However, the congestion costs are **internal** to road users as a group, since congestion is a cost largely borne by road users themselves in the form of increased time, fuel and other operating costs. Consequently this means that the issue of cost recovery does not arise in the same way as it does with infrastructure costs, since road infrastructure costs need to be covered either by funding from government or from toll revenues or from a combination of both. This funding issue does not arise with congestion.

Given the nature of congestion, which varies with traffic levels, and hence by both type of road and time of day, it is also not appropriate to calculate a single figure for the marginal congestion cost caused by a particular type of vehicle, such as a car or a heavy goods vehicle, since marginal congestion costs caused by different types of vehicle will vary across the highway network.

Consequently, our main objective is to quantify marginal congestion costs in the different member states, and to show how they will vary with actual traffic flows on different types of road. This reflects the fact that optimal charges will also need to vary according to expected traffic conditions.

---

[26]   International Energy Agency: Energy Prices and Taxes (Quarterly), OECD.

Although we focus in this study on marginal congestion costs (as reasoned above) we will also present results for total congestion costs for some countries for which the necessary data were available. The total congestion costs were mostly derived from estimating time losses within traffic-jams reported by police. Due to this, definitions and measurement are not comparable from country to country which holds therefore true also for the results presented.

3.6.3.2 *Measuring marginal congestion costs on Europe's roads*

In order to achieve our objective we have constructed a model to calculate marginal congestion costs, that is to say the additional congestion costs caused by an extra vehicle driving along a particular type of road for a given distance of one kilometre. As it will become clear from the model description following below, our approach is to estimate standardised marginal costs for each country varying only time values and some special characteristics. The model is constructed in such a way which allows to feed in (and to vary) other important input data if they are available such as country-specific speed-flow functions, flow data etc.

The model charts how marginal congestion costs will vary with traffic flow on different types of road in each member state. The results are summarised in chapter 4.

The model has been constructed as follows. It is based on the marginal congestion cost equation in formula (8) and (10) above. However, we have simplified the model to deal with two vehicle types, cars/light vans and heavy goods vehicles. The relationship between the extra congestion caused by an additional car or light van, and the extra congestion caused by an additional heavy goods vehicle, is given by the PCU (passenger car unit) value for a heavy goods vehicle, which can be specified by the model user. The impact of an extra vehicle on congestion will also depend on the proportion of heavy goods vehicles in the traffic flow: this proportion can also be specified in the model for any particular type of road in any country.

We now consider the other components of the model in more detail. **Speed-flow curves** are basically engineering relationships between traffic flows and speeds on different types of road, and we expect these engineering relations to be broadly similar across countries. Consequently we have used speed-flow relationships for a number of different types of road based on British experience.[27]

There is a straightforward (inverse) relationship between **speed** and the amount of **travel time**, and so travel time has been valued at values used for cars and goods vehicles in each member state, where such values are available. Where they were

---

[27] The model could be developed in the future to incorporate speed-flow relationships developed for other countries.

not, we have used travel time values related to average hourly earnings in those countries. Table A 17 in annex A provides detailed listings of the values available to the present study and therefore used in the model.

Our review of previous studies of congestion costs indicates that travel time appears to account for about 90 per cent of total congestion costs.[28] Of the remaining congestion costs, extra fuel is the largest component. The model uses actual prices of petrol and diesel in member states to value changes in fuel consumption. These values are shown in table A 17 in annex A too.

The physical changes in fuel consumption are based on British speed-fuel consumption formulae. While there may be some differences between fuel consumption by an average car and an average goods vehicle between different member states, we believe that the differences in fuel prices - which are taken into account in the model - will be more significant. In addition, it should be remembered that fuel consumption changes are a relatively small part of overall marginal congestion costs, given that, as we have noted above, such marginal congestion costs are dominated by increases in travel time rather than by changes in operating costs.

3.7 Summary: methodology proposed for this study

As the review of the state of the art and the detailed methodological discussion showed, the situation of road cost accounts within Europe is heterogeneous. This concerns the methodological approaches used, the availability and quality of data, and the frequency of data and studies elaborated. In general we can distinguish between three groups of countries: The first group comprises countries like Germany, Austria, Denmark, Finland, the UK, Sweden and Switzerland with a good database and sophisticated approaches. To the second group belong countries such as France, Ireland, the Netherlands and Spain with a good database but no sophisticated methodology. We count also Belgium to this group because at least long investment time series and expenditure data are available. The third group consists of the remaining EU-countries which have to our current information only a few sporadic estimates and no methodology of their own.

This grouping of countries has different methodological implications for road accounts. In general we consider it as more worthwhile to concentrate on the methodological issues of cost calculation and to define thoroughly the necessary methodological approaches and procedures including the required data, than to produce cost figures with sophisticated methods but poor databases. Furthermore, we prefer not to focus too much on standardisation/ harmonisation procedures

---

[28] This proportion will not, of course, be independent of the value of a unit of travel time.

since standardised data are hardly available and national specialities have to be considered. However, we see need for harmonisation concerning some basic principles of calculations for the future which we will - without getting into details - briefly discuss in chapter 5. Given the time constraints of this study we consider it as an important step to define the requirements for standardised minimal data collection on the EU-level (see again chapter 5). This general approach means:

1. For countries of group 1 we will base the empirical work on their own methodologies. The impacts of the different assumptions on the empirical results will be compared within sensitivity analyses. The findings both of the empirical work per country and of the sensitivity analyses will be used to choose and/or to elaborate methods for the other countries.

2. For the countries of group 2 the database allows to adopt a rather detailed method based on the methodological inputs from the first group.

3. Since the database for countries belonging to group 3 is not sufficient we can only roughly estimate capital values. Thus, we will produce just some illustrative figures which should not be overinterpreted.

Based on this general approach we define the following steps with different treatment of the country groups:

1. Definition of cost types

The most important methodological issue for infrastructure cost calculations is to distinguish between fixed, variable and marginal costs on the one hand and running cost and capital cost (i.e. capitalisation of annual investment expenditures) on the other hand. Since in many countries investment expenditures show considerable annual fluctuations, expenditure accounts are not the appropriate approach. Thus, we will apply a method which distinguishes between variable, marginal and fixed costs. This implies that capital costs have to be derived from a capital value for road infrastructure. It requires furthermore to estimate the shares of variable, marginal and fixed costs for those countries for which such data are not available. For countries with too poor database to estimate capital values and to derive capital costs we suggest concentrating on the estimation of marginal costs as parts of variable costs.

2. Definition of road types

We will consider the overall road network (excluding forest roads) and will provide also empirical results for motorways separately (as far as the data situation allows).

3. Vehicle classification

In this study we define the following categories as HGV:

- rigid goods vehicles (lorries with max. GVW > 3.5 t without trailer);

- lorries with trailer (including ordinary tractors with trailer, except agricultural vehicles);

- articulated vehicles (tractors with semi-trailer).

Buses and coaches as well as special vehicles and agricultural vehicles are excluded.

4. Estimation of capital values and capital costs

For those countries which already apply an own method for calculating capital values we base our study on these own methods without any harmonisation of model structures. For these countries we also apply the respective methods for depreciations and interests, i.e. the annuity method (e.g. Austria) or the depreciation/interest calculation within the perpetual inventory method (e.g. Germany, Denmark, Switzerland).

For those countries which do not have any estimates on road capital values up to now we will use two approaches:

- For countries like the UK, Ireland, Belgium, the Netherlands and Spain, which have longer investment time series (at least for 30 years) we apply a simplified perpetual inventory method. This concerns also the depreciation method within the perpetual inventory model and the respective calculation of interests.

- For countries without any sufficiently long investment time series, only rough estimates on the basis of indicators such as km-values in comparable countries are possible.[29] Here we will apply the annuity method. We consider this as a practicable way because it is not sensible to apply sophisticated depreciation methods to capital values which are only roughly estimated.

As far as interests are concerned, a real interest rate derived from the whole capital value according to the cost of governmental loans should be applied. If the capital value can not be evaluated at replacement costs (for example due to missing price indices for road construction), a second best method is applying a nominal interest rate on the capital value at purchase costs. VAT will be excluded as far as the data situation allows to do so.

---

[29]   More appropriate and thoroughly elaborated capital values for these contries would require a direct evaluation of road capital stocks. These countries should carry out such inventories of road assets in the future (as done in Denmark and Finland). The results could then easily be updated by applying the perpetual inventory method.

5. Non-transport related functions

We will consider the cost shares of these functions by percentages per road type. The values used in Switzerland and Austria might serve as a basis. However, national special conditions (such as a high proportion of non-motorised traffic in the Netherlands) will be considered.

6. Cost allocation

Based on the findings of the methodological comparison in section 3.4.3 we will use an approach with the following characteristics:

- Division of road infrastructure cost into:
  - Fixed cost (Cost shares of capital and running cost). These costs will be considered as capacity cost.
  - Variable cost.
- Application of three cost allocation factors for these cost categories:
  - Capacity costs: Allocation according to vkm and equivalent factors
  - Variable costs: Allocation according to standard axles-km, and vkm.

The equivalent factors have to be defined (speed /length-dependent) and may vary from country to country.

- For those countries which already apply an own method of cost allocation, their method is defined as the basic calculation. Other methods will be used for sensitivity analysis.
- For all other countries, the use of allocation factors should be transparent and should allow to consider special country features. Because of the considerable impacts of different methods, it is necessary to be flexible in choosing weight dependent cost shares.

7. Estimation of marginal costs

As explained in section 3.5 the current empirical situation in Europe requires a pragmatic approach. We consider the following categories as marginal costs:

- parts of maintenance expenditures for bridges/tunnels
- maintenance expenditures for pavement and resurfacing
- parts of reconstruction expenditures.

The shares of these cost items will be chosen in a flexible way considering national conditions (both regarding traffic-situation and data availability). Thus, they will vary from country to country. Further research is urgently required for the field of estimating marginal infrastructure costs.

8. Congestion costs

The general remarks made at the start of this chapter hold even more true for the congestion costs. Since the methodological situation and the database is even poorer than for infrastructure costs in the narrow sense we will concentrate more on elaborating thoroughly defined methodological steps and on formulating the necessary data-requirements. As outlined in chapter 3.6.3.2 we will produce standardised marginal congestion costs for each country, varying only the time values, fuel prices and some special characteristics. The model is constructed to allow for filling in further country-specific information such as speed-flow functions, traffic flow data and data on traffic structure.

Furthermore, we will provide results on total congestion costs for some countries based on available studies and data. Due to different methodological features, different definitions and data-sets these results are not comparable. However, we consider it nevertheless useful as an information and illustration provided the reader will treat the figures carefully.

4 Results

It is to our knowledge the first time that for all EU-countries a genuine road infrastructure cost calculation including a cost allocation to vehicle types was elaborated. The same is true for the estimation of marginal congestion costs. This chapter discusses the results which are also compiled as summarising tables for European countries in annex A. All figures for infrastructure costs are evaluated in ECU (ppp) by using the purchasing power parities/EKS method. For congestion costs a similar evaluation would require us to evaluate the values of travel time in detail. For example, a decision on which purchasing power parities (type of final expenditures) have to be applied would require to know the share of driving purposes. Therefore, we resigned to use the purchasing power parities for the congestion costs.

It should be noted in advance that the different methodological practices and the data availability restrict the comparability of results. Figure 11 shows the most important factors which influence the comparability of empirical results. These are on the one hand the national conditions summarised under the three keywords economic conditions, road network and transport characteristics, as well as the practice of road maintenance. These are factors reflecting the different „reality" in the EU-countries. On the other hand, different methodological philosophies (calculation of capital values, cost allocation procedures) and different definitions and delimitations (definition of the road network, delimitation between investments and maintenance) are important. Furthermore, the availability and quality of data (for example lacking data which had to be supplemented by own estimates) are reasons why the results are not fully comparable and should not be overinterpreted.

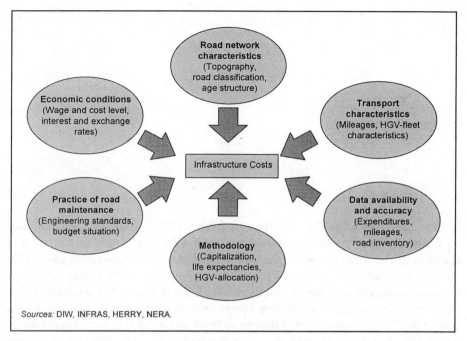

Figure 11: Factors influencing the comparability of national infrastructure cost accounts

4.1 Capital values and road infrastructure costs

The figures 12 - 17 show the km-specific results for the net capital value, the capital costs, the costs of motorised traffic and the costs of HGV. They were estimated for the total road network and for the motorways. However, for the motorways only results for a few countries are available.

1. Net capital value

   As can be seen from figure 12, there is a group of countries with high net capital values per km of total network. To this group belong France (with the highest value at a considerable distance to the other EU-countries), Germany, Austria, Switzerland, Luxembourg and also Finland. Looking at the results for motorways in figure 13, the ranking of countries changed. Here Switzerland shows the highest value per km, followed by France, Austria and Germany. A cautious interpretation of these results has to consider the following issues:

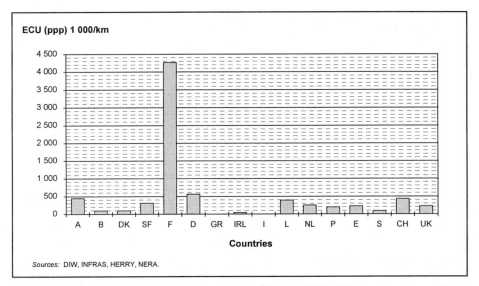

Figure 12: Net capital value of roads in Europe 1994 in 1000 ECU (ppp) per km - Total road network -

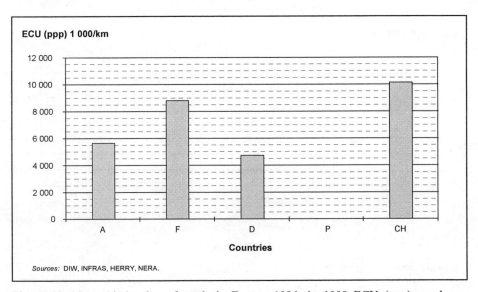

Figure 13: Net capital value of roads in Europe 1994, in 1000 ECU (ppp) per km - Motorways -

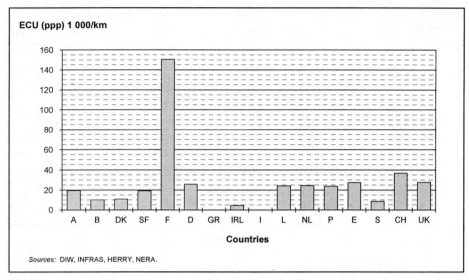

Figure 14: Capital costs of roads in Europe 1994, in 1000 ECU (ppp) per km - Total road network -

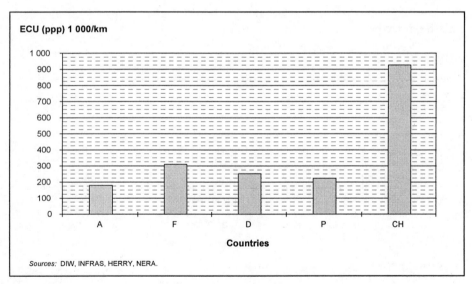

Figure 15: Capital costs of roads in Europe 1994, in 1000 ECU (ppp) per km - Motorways -

- In general, the differences between the net capital value per km among the EU-countries are on the one hand caused by „real world" characteristics such as different investment history, maintenance cycles and practices, construction standards/quality and age structure. On the other hand methodological impacts (approach for estimation of capital values, parameters used) play an important role.

- Another influencing factor is the type and quality of input data. For those capital values derived with the perpetual inventory method, the investment time series[30] are most important. Here, the national practice regarding the definition/delimitation of investments, maintenance and other expenditures is rather heterogeneous. Particularly the different definitions of investments and maintenance obviously applied in the EC-countries cause serious problems if a capital value is to be calculated with the perpetual inventory concept as done for most countries within this project.

- The comparability is also restricted by the fact that for some countries the figures refer to parts of the network only (Spain, Portugal, France).

- The figure for France contains the capital value for concessioned motorways which are operated privately. This capital value is derived from entrepreneurial balance-sheets and is thus not comparable with the capital value for the roads of other countries mentioned above (compare section 3.3.1.3).

- The capital values for Switzerland and Denmark are figures in nominal terms. They are thus not directly comparable with the other results.

- Although the figures are derived from different methodological concepts (synthetic method for Austria and Finland, perpetual inventory concept for the other countries mentioned above) no correlation can be found to show that in general one method leads to higher values than the other. High capital values are also caused by high investments in the past and - for Germany and Switzerland for example - by high construction and labour costs (high construction standards).

---

[30]   Tables A 3 and A 4 in annex A show the development of road investment in Europe during the last 10 years.

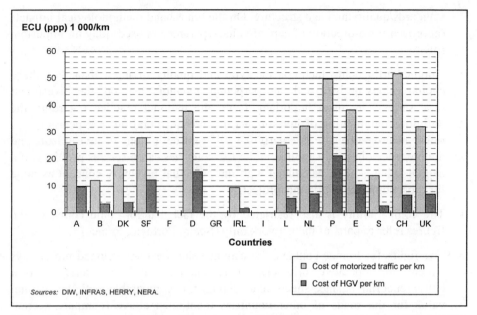

Figure 16: Costs of motorised traffic and costs of HGV for roads in Europe 1994, in 1000 ECU (ppp) per km - Total road network -

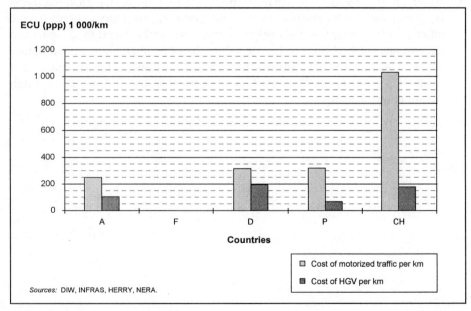

Figure 17: Costs of motorised traffic and costs of HGV for roads in Europe 1994, in 1000 ECU (ppp) per km - Motorways -

2. Capital costs

The highest capital costs per km total road network were calculated for France (see figure 14). However, this value should not be overinterpreted due to the problems already mentioned under point 1. Other countries with high capital charges per km are apart from Switzerland also the UK, Spain and Germany. Explanations for the different cost levels are on the one hand methodic differences such as

– lower capital costs yielded with the annuity method (applied for Austria and France) in comparison with the perpetual inventory concept and

– consideration of the age structure of assets calculated with the perpetual inventory concept (in contrast to the annuity method).

On the other hand these differences reflect reality in the levels of costs expressed in different life expectancies of assets, different interest rates applied and also in the frequency and quality of maintenance.

The results for the motorways (figure 15) show the highest capital costs for Switzerland, followed with considerable distance by France, Germany, Portugal and Austria.

3. Road infrastructure costs

The problems of interpreting the results properly mentioned above hold true for the costs of motorised traffic and of HGVs (figures 16 and 17) as well. It has also to be borne in mind that the total infrastructure costs were not for all countries diminished by the costs of non-transport related road functions and the costs of non-motorised traffic.

The costs of motorised traffic per km and those related to HGV vary considerably. While for the total road network Switzerland shows the highest costs of motorised traffic per km, it ranks only at the fifth place regarding the HGV costs. This is caused by the ton-limit for HGV in Switzerland on the one hand and by the HGV-friendly cost allocation method on the other hand. Apart from Switzerland, the costs of motorised traffic are high in Portugal, Spain and Germany. Concerning the HGV-related costs Portugal, Germany and Finland rank at the top.

Also for the motorways Switzerland shows the highest value regarding the costs of all motorised traffic while the HGV-costs are lower than those for Germany. Of course a genuine European comparison for the costs of motorways is not possible since there are only results for four countries available.

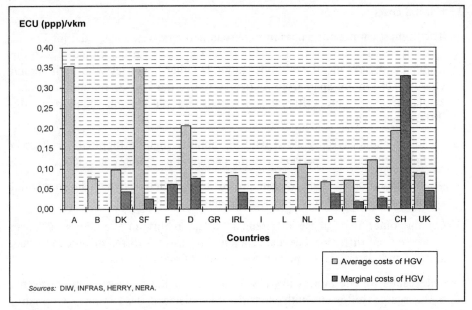

Figure 18: Average and marginal costs of HGV for roads in Europe 1994 - Total road network -

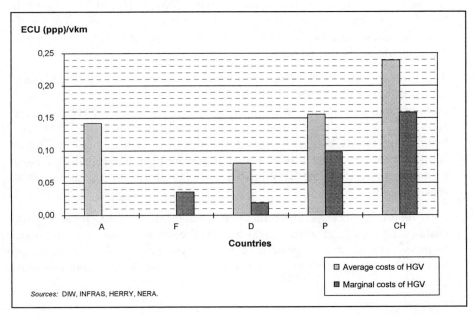

Figure 19: Average and marginal costs of HGV for roads in Europe 1994 - Motorways -

4.2 Average and marginal road infrastructure costs

Figures 18 and 19 present the results for average and marginal infrastructure costs of HGV per vehicle-km. As far as the data allowed, the figures were calculated both for the total road network and for the motorways. The variety of results is quite high and it should be noted in advance that the estimation of marginal infrastructure costs is complicated.

Related to HGVs the average costs per vehicle-km driven at the total road network are the highest in Austria, Finland and Germany followed by Switzerland. Although an interpretation is complicated by different it can be stated that particularly the high costs in Austria, Germany and Switzerland are caused by the high costs of road construction in general. Marginal costs per vehicle-km could be derived for Denmark, Finland, France, Germany, Ireland, Portugal (only HGV), Spain, Sweden, Switzerland and the UK. Here Switzerland ranks at the top with the phenomenon that the marginal costs even exceed the average costs.[31] From the remaining countries, Germany and France lay at the upper bound while Spain shows the lowest value.

Concerning motorways there are only results for five countries available. Here we can observe that the relation between average and marginal costs for Switzerland turns in comparison to the same relation for the total road network. Switzerland ranks for both values at the top, followed by Portugal.

4.3 Congestion costs

There are only a few countries for which total congestion costs could be estimated (Austria, Germany, Portugal, Switzerland, UK) or collected from existing studies (The Netherlands, Ireland and Spain). The results are contained in table 21. First of all it should be mentioned that the figures given in table 21 were derived from different methodological concepts. For example, the figures for Ireland, Spain and the UK are based on a modelling approach in which actual traffic conditions are compared with hypothetical „free flow" conditions. The figures for the other countries were calculated by using police reports on traffic delays. Furthermore, the road network taken into account varies among the countries. For Ireland and Spain only figures for Dublin and Madrid are available. To this adds the problem, that available data and/or studies concern different years. Due to these problems

---

[31]   It should be borne in mind that the marginal costs calculated for Switzerland are not genuine marginal costs but contain parts of investive maintenance and running expenditures. Doubtless, more in-depth analysis is required in order to clarify the Swiss results. This holds true particularly, if such results are to be used for a marginal cost pricing.

and differences, the results are hardly comparable and serve more as a general information and illustration.

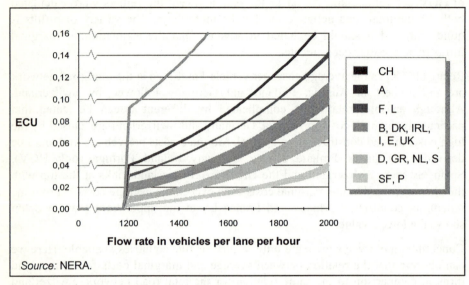

Figure 20: Marginal congestion costs 1994: Interurban motorways - Passenger cars -

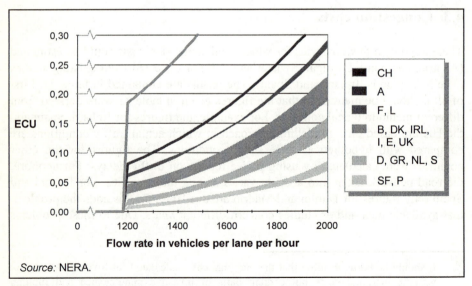

Figure 21: Marginal congestion costs 1994: Interurban motorways - Goods vehicles -

Figures 20 and 21 summarise the marginal congestion cost curves derived with the modelling approach from section 3.6 for the interurban motorways. We grouped the congestion cost curves yielded for each country in order to obtain bands of curves. Similar curve bands can also be obtained for the other road types considered in our study. However, we do not present them in this chapter since the shape of curves and the country grouping are the same as shown in figures 20 and 21. As can be seen there, Switzerland ranks at the top, followed by Austria and a group containing France and Luxembourg while Finland and Portugal form a group with low marginal congestion costs.

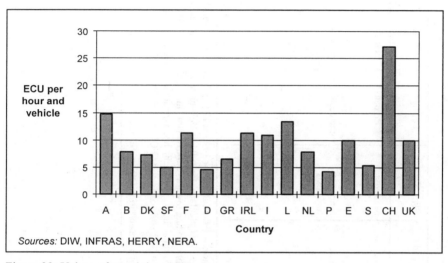

Figure 22: Values of travel time 1994 - Passenger cars -

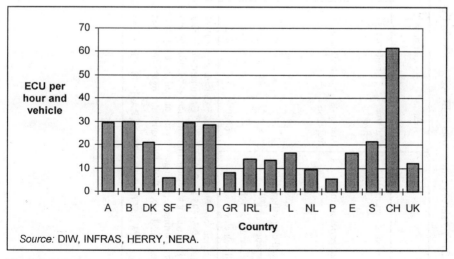

Figure 23: Values of travel time 1994 - Goods vehicles -

Table 21: Total congestion costs in EU-countries - in ECU mill. -

	Austria[1]	Germany[2]	Ireland[3]	The Netherlands[4]	Portugal[5]	Spain[6]	Switzerland[7]	United Kingdom[8]
Road network concerned	total road network	motorways[9]	Dublin only	Main roads[10]	Main roads	Madrid only	Motorways and urban traffic	Total road network
Cost categories included	time costs fuel costs	time costs	time costs	time costs fuel costs	time costs	time costs fuel costs other operating costs	time costs	time costs fuel costs other operating costs
Estimated congestion costs								
Passenger cars[11]		131			176		537	8031
Heavy goods vehicles[12]		141			27		62	481
All vehicles	6620[13]	272	630	662	203	1350[14]	599	8512

[1] Calculated for 1994 at 1994 prices. - [2] Calculated for 1994 at 1994 prices. - [3] Calculated for 1994 at 1994 prices. - [4] Calculated for 1996 at 1996 prices. - [5] Calculated for 1996 at 1996 prices. - [6] Calculated for 1995 at 1995 prices. - [7] Calculated for 1992 at 1992 prices. - [8] Calculated for 1994 at 1994 prices. - [9] Only traffic jams with interregional importance. - [10] Traffic jams and „situations tending towards a traffic jam" included. - [11] Includes passenger cars and light goods vehicles. Germany: passenger cars and mopeds/motorcycles included. Portugal: light goods vehicles, agricultural vehicles and special vehicles included. - [12] Goods vehicles. Germany: also light goods vehicles included. - [13] Time costs only: ECU mill. 6170. - [14] Time costs only: ECU mill. 1215.

Sources: DIW, INFRAS, HERRY, NERA, ECIS, Theiss Consult, Dublin Transportation Office, NEA, BRISA, Monzon and Villanueva 1995.

Due to the fact that we used a harmonised methodology to estimate marginal congestion costs, these results are easier to compare than those for infrastructure costs in the narrow sense. The main differences between the countries stem from the levels of time values on the one hand and specifications of the road network on the other hand.

Most important are the values of travel time applied for our calculations. They are shown in the figures 22 and 23. It should be noted that not all of these values have a status as the official values. Furthermore, since the time values stem from sources with different definitions, it is not in all cases clear what they do include. These effects are difficult to separate from the levels of time values which do indeed reflect differences in reality. For example, regarding the values of travel time for passenger cars, Portugal, Germany and Finland have the lowest values while Switzerland ranks at the top. For goods vehicles the variety of values is even larger. Here we can distinguish between high-cost countries (Switzerland, then followed by a considerable distance by Austria, Belgium, France and Germany) and a low-cost group containing Portugal, Finland, the Netherlands and Greece. The differences in the marginal congestion cost curves are mainly caused by these different time values.

5 Conclusions and recommendations

5.1 Towards a harmonised methodology

5.1.1 General remarks

Within this study,

- the existing practice of infrastructure cost accounting and estimation of congestion costs in the countries of the European Union and Switzerland was analysed,

- the relevant methodological issues were discussed, and the respective national practices were quantitatively compared, and

- empirical results for heavy goods vehicles - based on available data and existing methodology - were presented.

We have seen that the practice in European countries is heterogeneous. Consequently, the comparability of empirical results is restricted. However, the study was able to improve the knowledge on sensitive parameters, especially for the procedures to estimate capital values and costs, for the cost allocation to different type of vehicles and for the values of time needed for congestion cost estimates. The respective comparative analysis (applied for some countries) in chapter 3 is therefore of particular importance in order to propose further steps towards a harmonised methodology.

A harmonised method has to respect the national situation. Most important are the status of road organisation (institutional background, road classification), road network features and traffic characteristics, the national economic situation and - last but not least - the existing practice and data availability. From this point of view it is not a harmonised method in the narrow sense which is required, but a harmonised methodological framework. This framework requires:

1. Periodical results for important indicators (see section 5.1.2, paragraph a)

2. Minimal standards for a harmonised procedure to estimate these results (see section 5.1.2, paragraph b)

3. Specific additional information, if these results have direct political importance (for example appropriate pricing of specific corridors or taxation for road use) (see section 5.1.2, paragraph c).

5.1.2 Proposition for a harmonised methodological framework

a) Which periodical results?

The methodic analysis as well as the empirical work in this study have shown clearly that the following data and results have to be provided for and within road cost accounts:

- **Annual road expenditures** are an essential information required as input data for calculating infrastructure costs.

- **Infrastructure capital values** are the basis to derive **capital costs**, which are a relevant part of total infrastructure costs.

- **Data on mileages** driven by the different vehicle types are necessary in order to break down total costs of motorised traffic to vehicle types. If these data are lacking, none of the cost categories mentioned below can be calculated.

- **Marginal infrastructure costs per type of vehicle** can be used for efficient pricing of HGV per km of non congested roads.

- **Marginal congestion costs per type of vehicle** are important for efficient pricing of congested roads. It should be noted that charging marginal congestion costs has to consider both HGVs and other types of vehicles. Since it is rather complicated to transfer the marginal cost curves into practice, they have to be simplified. For this simplification it is necessary to classify the existing road network into different categories (e.g. different levels of traffic volume) and to apply a limited number of different prices according to the traffic volume per hour (e.g. high peak, pre-peak, after-peak, no congestion). This simplification should be a rather pragmatic one since it is difficult to anticipate user responses to congestion pricing.

- **Average infrastructure costs per type of vehicle** are not directly price relevant, but are important for the issues of cost recovery and fair allocation of fixed costs. A detailed allocation has to consider the above mentioned marginal costs component in order to avoid double counting

- The results for **total congestion costs** are not price relevant either. Nevertheless, they provide relevant information about the welfare losses within the road transport sector.

Periodical information on these indicators would be very helpful for the EC-Commission in order to compare the trends and structure of road costs in the member states and for justifying specific price schemes. However, it has to be stated that the expense of time and labour to produce this information is very high. Given the experience with the EC infrastructure regulation from 1970, annual information on all indicators on a very detailed level might not be appropriate. From our point of view, the essential data which are to be collected on an annual basis should comprise:

- road expenditures, divided into investment, maintenance, and other; and

- kilometres driven by different vehicle types.

In addition, a road inventory should be carried out for one reference year which can serve as a basis for estimating the road capital value (initial value). This value can then easily be updated by using the annual road investments. We propose that these data should be integrated into the annual EUROSTAT-publications. Detailed information on the cost categories mentioned above (average and marginal infrastructure costs by vehicle types, marginal congestion costs, total congestion costs) have to be requested by the Commission, if countries intend to introduce new pricing schemes, which affect international transport flows.

b) Harmonised methodological framework

1. Definition of cost types

Since annual investment expenditures show considerable annual fluctuations in many countries, expenditure accounts are not appropriate both under theoretical and practical aspects. Thus, a method which distinguishes variable, marginal and fixed costs and which estimates capital costs out of a capital value for road infrastructure should be applied.

2. Definition of road types

It is at least necessary to distinguish between motorways and the remaining national road network. Additional information on regional and municipal roads would be useful, but due to the difficult data situation in most countries it is not practicable for the EC-Commission to oblige the member states for reporting these data frequently.

3. Vehicle classification

Regarding traffic data for HGVs, it is necessary to distinguish at least between:

- Rigid goods vehicles (lorries with max. GVW > 3.5 t without trailer);

- Lorries with trailer (including ordinary tractors with trailer except agricultural vehicles);

- Articulated vehicles (tractors with semi-trailer).

A further differentiation of HGV-related data into different weight categories would be useful. Further information on vehicle categories such as passenger cars, buses and light goods vehicles are essential, if HGV costs are to be separated out from total costs and if the costs of these other categories are to be identified.

4. Estimation of capital values and capital costs

According to the availability of national data, either the estimation of capital values and capital costs with the perpetual inventory method (based on sufficiently long expenditure time series) or with the synthetic method (based on a detailed inventory of the existing network by asset types, use of the annuity method for the capital costs) is appropriate. The values should include land values and exclude general taxes such as VAT, unless institutional characteristics (e.g. private motorways) justify another practice. If possible a calculation in real terms (based on constant prices and real interest rates) should be presented. If not possible, a calculation in nominal terms (based on current prices and nominal interest rates) is a second best solution.

The following parameters should be based on the respective national conditions:

- Expected lifetime, if possible by asset types, based on country specific empirical studies,

- Interest rates based on opportunity costs of governmental loans and applied for the total capital value.

5. Non-transport related functions

The cost allocation by type of vehicle should consider non transport related functions of the road network as well as the costs of non-motorised traffic. This holds true especially for the regional and municipal road network. The percentages should be based on national characteristics.

6. Cost allocation

A detailed harmonised method cannot be recommended, since national features have to be considered. Therefore, we propose a **transparent** procedure which takes the following issues into account:

- The road infrastructure cost should be divided into:

  - Fixed cost (cost shares of capital and running cost) which are considered as capacity cost, and

  - Variable cost, depending on the mileage driven by type of vehicles.

- For these cost categories three cost allocation factors[32] should be applied:

  - For capacity costs we propose an allocation according to vkm and/or specific equivalence factors. Percentages to consider special road designs (especially for large and heavy vehicles) might be applied in addition.

  - Variable costs should be allocated according to standard axles-km and vkm.

The equivalent factors have to be defined concerning their basis (speed /length-dependent, based on PCU's) and their value. They may vary from country to country. The same is true for the standard axles which are used to allocate weight dependent variable costs according to country-specific road designs.

7. Marginal infrastructure costs

As already discussed in this study the problem of how to estimate marginal infrastructure costs in a theoretically adequate and practicable way has not yet been solved in the EU-countries. Further research in this field is urgently required. Against this background we propose as a first approach to distinguish at least the following cost categories as a basis for estimating marginal costs:

- parts of maintenance expenditures for bridges/tunnels,

- maintenance expenditures for pavement and resurfacing,

- parts of reconstruction expenditures.

For the allocation of marginal costs by type of vehicles, specific and transparent assumptions should be made. We propose a similar allocation method as for the variable costs. However, also for this area further research is necessary to propose a more detailed methodology.

8. Congestion costs

- Time values:

  The time values should take into account national conditions such as the economic situation and especially the national wage levels. It should be ensured that they are delimitated for all member states according to common principles.

- Marginal congestion costs:

  Marginal congestion costs should take into account the traffic volume by type of vehicle, different user segments (i.e. commuters, business and leisure) and the type of road (capacity). General recommendations do not seem to be

---

[32] Vehicle-km, equivalence factors, standard axles-km.

appropriate. We regard the standardised approach presented in this study as a useful starting point but have to state that further research is needed.

- Total congestion costs:

  They require detailed information on bottlenecks and time losses for different road categories. The estimations should be based on national transport model simulations or on empirical surveys.

c) Additional information/Sensitivity analysis

If countrywise cost results are requested for specific questions such as justifying the introduction of new pricing schemes, further information on the background of specific assumptions and on the sensitivity of the results would be very useful. This is true especially for the most sensitive parameters which are, according to the analysis in this report:

- the method applied to estimate capital values,

- the life expectancy by type of asset,

- the method applied for cost allocation (in particular: assumptions on weight dependent costs),

- the volume of traffic (vkm, number of vehicles) of specific roads.

5.2 Further research needs

The study has shown that further research on several gaps identified within the analysis is required. This study dealt especially with HGVs but the gaps in methodologies and data refer to other types of vehicles too. In our point of view further research is needed in the following fields:

- More international empirical evidence on the economic lifetime of different types of assets is necessary.

- The different approaches for capital values in entrepreneurial balance-sheets and for public-owned infrastructure require detailed analysis.

- General investigations in countries with an insufficient database have to be carried out. This concerns most of all expenditure time series, road network inventories and data on traffic performance.

- In-depth analysis of marginal infrastructure costs by type of vehicles are required, both from an economical/empirical and an engineering point of view.

- In addition to running research projects, internationally comparable time values in Europe should be elaborated.

- Marginal congestion costs have to be analysed more deeply, based on a sophisticated model approach.

- More detailed investigations and propositions need to be elaborated for specific types of infrastructure: Infrastructure in environmentally sensitive areas and/or areas with complicated construction conditions are characterised by higher cost levels with different cost structures (e.g. alpine transit).

- Other external costs such as external accident costs and external environmental costs should be considered.

Annex A - Summarising tables

Table A 1: Total road expenditures in Europe in ECU mill., at current prices - Total road network -

Year	A[1]	B	DK	SF[2]	F	D	GR	IRL	I	L	NL	P[3]	E[4]	S	CH	UK[5]
1984	1 095	950	826	705	n.a.	10 601	n.a.	353	n.a.	102	2 618	85	n.a.	n.a.	2 362	n.a.
1985	1 138	814	944	772	n.a.	11 253	n.a.	412	n.a.	103	2 704	100	n.a.	n.a.	2 230	n.a.
1986	1 172	588	879	786	n.a.	12 263	n.a.	428	n.a.	107	2 689	135	n.a.	n.a.	2 513	n.a.
1987	1 050	658	858	860	n.a.	12 814	n.a.	365	n.a.	123	2 925	157	n.a.	880	2 633	n.a.
1988	1 026	633	842	916	n.a.	12 994	n.a.	343	n.a.	143	2 854	175	n.a.	996	2 795	n.a.
1989	987	372	846	1 055	n.a.	13 434	n.a.	407	n.a.	171	2 953	198	n.a.	1 281	2 815	n.a.
1990	1 064	576	819	1 131	n.a.[6]	13 956	n.a.	461	n.a.	126	2 889	293	n.a.	1 331	3 226	n.a.
1991	956	590	880	1 237	n.a.	13 296	n.a.	490	n.a.	148	2 839	360	n.a.	1 385	3 635	n.a.
1992	1 007	616	919	1 057	n.a.	22 443	n.a.	524	n.a.	161	2 876	483	n.a.	1 518	3 463	n.a.
1993	970	691	1 018	852	n.a.	22 691	n.a.	604	n.a.	237	2 571	479	n.a.	1 614	3 681	n.a.
1994	1 049	730	1 092	927	n.a.	23 207	n.a.	559	n.a.	231	2 966	575	5 618	2 032	3 863	7 934

[1] Motorways, expressways and trunk roads only. - [2] Public road network only. - [3] National road network only. - [4] National road network only, without motorways. - [5] Financial year 1 April to 31 March. - [6] According to Brossier (1996) the total road expenditures in France 1990 amounted to 11 629 ECU mill.

Sources: EU-Commission, national transport ministries, CEMT, IRF, national motorway companies, estimations of DIW, INFRAS, HERRY, NERA.

Table A 2: Total road expenditures in Europe in ECU mill., at current prices - Motorways -

Year	A	B	DK	SF	F	D	GR	IRL	I	L	NL[1]	P[2]	E	S	CH	UK
1984	550	n.a.	110	n.a.	n.a.	1 385	n.a.	n.a.	n.a.	n.a.	417	n.a.	n.a.	n.a.	749	n.a.
1985	562	n.a.	103	n.a.	n.a.	1 410	n.a.	n.a.	n.a.	n.a.	434	n.a.	n.a.	n.a.	712	n.a.
1986	574	n.a.	85	n.a.	n.a.	1 462	n.a.	n.a.	n.a.	n.a.	585	n.a.	n.a.	n.a.	706	n.a.
1987	497	n.a.	79	n.a.	n.a.	1 580	n.a.	n.a.	n.a.	n.a.	514	n.a.	n.a.	n.a.	740	n.a.
1988	487	n.a.	86	n.a.	n.a.	1 643	n.a.	n.a.	n.a.	n.a.	844	n.a.	n.a.	n.a.	809	n.a.
1989	493	n.a.	100	n.a.	n.a.	1 662	n.a.	n.a.	n.a.	n.a.	887	n.a.	n.a.	n.a.	834	n.a.
1990	568	n.a.	107	n.a.	n.a.[3]	1 765	n.a.	n.a.	n.a.	n.a.	741	228	n.a.	n.a.	1 020	n.a.
1991	520	n.a.	135	n.a.	n.a.	2 218	n.a.	n.a.	n.a.	n.a.	712	313	n.a.	n.a.	1 188	n.a.
1992	499	n.a.	146	n.a.	n.a.	2 576	n.a.	n.a.	n.a.	n.a.	683	151	n.a.	n.a.	1 175	n.a.
1993	441	n.a.	144	n.a.	n.a.	3 041	n.a.	n.a.	n.a.	n.a.	752	239	n.a.	n.a.	1 400	n.a.
1994	447	n.a.	133	n.a.	n.a.	3 056	n.a.	n.a.	n.a.	n.a.	868	310	n.a.	n.a.	1 420	n.a.

[1] Since 1988 trunk roads (Rijkswegen which include motorways and other trunk roads). - [2] Only motorways run by BRISA. - [3] According to Brossier (1996) the total road expenditures for motorways in France 1990 amounted to 1 924 ECU mill.

Sources: EU-Commission, national transport ministries, CEMT, IRF, national motorway companies, estimations of DIW, INFRAS, HERRY, NERA.

Table A 3: Road investments in Europe in ECU mill., at current prices - Total road network -

Year	A[1]	B	DK	SF[2]	F	D	GR	IRL	I	L	NL	P[3]	E[4]	S	CH	UK[5]
1984	706	479	235	301	4 016	6 010	263	137	3 216	75	1 067	50	n.a.	n.a.	1 187	n.a.
1985	727	422	262	341	4 386	6 262	280	172	3 662	73	1 082	64	n.a.	482	1 179	4 071
1986	757	304	248	326	4 926	6 814	175	181	4 302	73	959	78	n.a.	446	1 269	3 708
1987	620	340	229	346	5 240	6 969	159	142	4 522	86	1 108	94	n.a.	464	1 325	3 894
1988	602	326	235	381	6 225	7 117	199	135	5 385	108	1 038	119	n.a.	532	1 376	4 645
1989	559	234	221	434	6 506	7 372	242	192	5 952	82	1 087	140	2 588	686	1 412	5 515
1990	590	295	180	529	6 957[6]	7 593	234	231	7 572	76	1 214	214	3 667	731	1 669	5 906
1991	520	304	172	753	7 328	6 592	254	250	8 132	109	1 193	294	4 277	684	1 920	6 181
1992	539	309	191	660	7 593	12 891	355	288	8 223	144	1 208	393	4 048	805	1 770	6 283
1993	471	357	232	564	8 291	12 784	456	369	6 400	219	1 312	349	3 856	996	1 935	5 992
1994	491	344	294	636	8 735	12 914	371	301	n.a.	214	1 529	445	3 816	1 014	2 037	5 949

[1] Motorways, expressways and trunk roads only. - [2] Public road network only. - [3] National road network only, without motorways. - [4] National road network only. - [5] Financial year 1 April to 31 March. - [6] According to Brossier (1996) the road investment expenditures in France 1990 amounted to 5 054 ECU mill.

Sources: EU-Commission, national transport ministries, CEMT, IRF, national motorway companies, estimations of DIW, INFRAS, HERRY, NERA.

Table A 4: Road investments in Europe in ECU mill., at current prices - Motorways -

Year	A	B	DK	SF	F	D	GR	IRL	I	L	NL[1]	P[2]	E	S	CH	UK
1984	399	n.a.	70	n.a.	n.a.	1 041	n.a.	n.a.	n.a.	n.a.	237	n.a.	n.a.	n.a.	657	n.a.
1985	402	n.a.	60	n.a.	n.a.	1 119	n.a.	n.a.	n.a.	n.a.	247	n.a.	n.a.	n.a.	604	n.a.
1986	410	n.a.	39	n.a.	n.a.	1 170	n.a.	n.a.	n.a.	n.a.	256	n.a.	n.a.	n.a.	554	n.a.
1987	328	n.a.	36	n.a.	n.a.	1 202	n.a.	n.a.	n.a.	n.a.	290	n.a.	n.a.	n.a.	552	n.a.
1988	324	n.a.	39	n.a.	n.a.	1 230	n.a.	n.a.	n.a.	n.a.	314	n.a.	n.a.	n.a.	575	n.a.
1989	331	n.a.	48	n.a.	n.a.	1 246	n.a.	n.a.	n.a.	n.a.	341	n.a.	n.a.	n.a.	598	n.a.
1990	376	n.a.	49	n.a.	n.a.[3]	1 301	n.a.	n.a.	n.a.	n.a.	379	210	n.a.	n.a.	750	n.a.
1991	329	n.a.	72	n.a.	n.a.	1 687	n.a.	n.a.	n.a.	n.a.	342	282	n.a.	n.a.	882	n.a.
1992	302	n.a.	78	n.a.	n.a.	2 059	n.a.	n.a.	n.a.	n.a.	283	116	n.a.	n.a.	856	n.a.
1993	236	n.a.	70	n.a.	n.a.	2 247	n.a.	n.a.	n.a.	n.a.	324	206	n.a.	n.a.	1 062	n.a.
1994	213	n.a.	65	n.a.	n.a.	2 218	n.a.	n.a.	n.a.	n.a.	469	271	n.a.	n.a.	1 098	n.a.

[1] Since 1988 trunk roads (Rijkswegen which include motorways and other trunk roads). - [2] Only motorways run by BRISA. - [3] According to Brossier (1996) the road investment expenditures for motorways in France 1990 amounted to 696 ECU mill.

Sources: EU-Commission, national transport ministries, CEMT, IRF, national motorway companies, estimations of DIW, INFRAS, HERRY, NERA.

Table A 5: Specific costs of roads in Europe 1994, in 1000 ECU per km, at 1994 prices - Total road network -

	A[1]	B	DK[2]	SF[3]	F[4]	D	GR	IRL	I	L	NL	P[5]	E[6]	S	CH[7]	UK[8]
Gross capital value per km[9][10]	n.a.	207	n.a.	n.a.	n.a.	835	n.a.	47	n.a.	680	541	n.a.	365	n.a.	n.a.	353
Net capital value per km[9][10]	441	94	101	220	4 387	636	n.a.	31	n.a.	450	295	98	215	105	468	202
Capital costs per km[11][12]	19.1	9.7	11.4	13.7	154.7	29.1	n.a.	3.3	n.a.	27.7	28.9	12.0	26.1	10.1	40.1	25.2
Running costs per km[13]	6.5	2.7	7.1	6.2	n.a.	16.4	n.a.	3.8	n.a.	3.2	13.7	13.1	11.2	7.5	16.1	5.4
Total infrastructure costs per km	25.6	12.4	18.4	19.9	n.a.	45.5	n.a.	7.1	n.a.	30.9	42.6	25.1	37.3	17.6	n.a.	30.6
Costs of motorised traffic per km	25.0	11.7	18.4	19.9	n.a.	42.7	n.a.	6.9	n.a.	29.1	38.2	25.1	36.6	16.6	56.2	29.2
Costs of HGV per km[14]	9.6	3.1	4.1	8.8	n.a.	17.3	n.a.	1.2	n.a.	6.2	8.4	10.7	10.0	3.1	7.3	6.4

[1] 1990 figures, at 1990 prices. - [2] At current prices. - [3] 1995 figures. Public road network only. - [4] 1995 figures, at 1995 prices. Motorways and trunk roads only. - [5] 1995 figures, at 1995 prices. Capital value: total road network. Costs: total road network. - [6] National road network without motorways. - [7] National road network only. - [8] Financial year 1 April 1994 to 31 March 1995. - [9] As at 31 December. Austria: there was no information to which reference day the data current prices. - [8] Financial year 1 April 1994 to 31 March 1995. - [10] Including land value. Finland: no information available. - [11] Calculated as refer. Luxembourg: rough estimates. United Kingdom: as at 31 March 1995. - [10] Including land value. Finland: no information available. Switzerland: only costs of road average over the year. Austria: there was no information to which reference period the data refer. Luxembourg: rough estimates. Switzerland: only costs of road use for transport related functions. United Kingdom: calculated as average over financial year. - [12] Including land costs. Finland: no information available. - [13] Switzerland: only costs of road use for transport related functions. - [14] Goods vehicles ≥ 3.5 t max. GVW. Austria: ≥ 4 t max. GVW. Denmark, Switzerland: ≥ 3 t max. GVW. Portugal: no information available.

Sources: DIW, INFRAS, HERRY, NERA.

Table A 6: Specific costs of roads in Europe 1994, in 1000 ECU (PPP) per km, at 1994 prices - Total road network -

	A[1]	B	DK[2]	SF[3]	F[4]	D	GR	IRL	I	L	NL	P[5]	E[6]	S	CH[7]	UK[8]
Gross capital value per km[9)10]	n.a.	217	n.a.	n.a.	n.a.	740	n.a.	65	n.a.	589	457	n.a.	382	n.a.	n.a.	389
Net capital value per km[9)10]	448	99	98	309	4 272	564	n.a.	43	n.a.	390	249	194	225	88	431	223
Capital costs per km[11)12]	19.4	10.1	11.0	19.2	150.6	25.8	n.a.	4.5	n.a.	24.0	24.4	23.8	27.3	8.5	36.9	27.7
Running costs per km[13]	6.6	2.8	6.8	8.7	n.a.	14.5	n.a.	5.2	n.a.	2.8	11.6	26.0	11.7	6.3	14.8	6.0
Total infrastructure costs per km	26.0	13.0	17.8	27.9	n.a.	40.3	n.a.	9.7	n.a.	26.8	36.0	49.7	39.1	14.8	n.a.	33.7
Costs of motorised traffic per km	25.4	12.2	17.8	27.9	n.a.	37.9	n.a.	9.4	n.a.	25.2	32.3	49.7	38.3	13.9	51.7	32.1
Costs of HGV per km[14]	9.7	3.3	4.0	12.3	n.a.	15.3	n.a.	1.6	n.a.	5.4	7.1	21.2	10.5	2.6	6.7	7.1

[1] 1990 figures, at 1990 prices. - [2] At current prices. - [3] 1995 figures. Public road network only. - [4] 1995 figures, at 1995 prices. Motorways and trunk roads only. - [5] 1995 figures, at 1995 prices. Capital value: total road network. Costs: national road network without motorways. - [6] National road network only. - [7] At current prices. - [8] Financial year 1 April 1994 to 31 March 1995. - [9] As at 31 December. Austria: there was no information to which reference day the data refer. Luxembourg: rough estimates. United Kingdom: as at 31 March 1995. - [10] Including land value. Finland: no information available. - [11] Calculated as average over the year. Austria: there was no information to which reference period the data refer. Luxembourg: rough estimates. Switzerland: only costs of road use for transport related functions. United Kingdom: calculated as average over financial year. - [12] Including land costs. Finland: no information available. - [13] Switzerland: only costs of road use for transport related functions. - [14] Goods vehicles ≥ 3.5 t max. GVW. Austria: ≥ 4 t max. GVW. Denmark, Switzerland: ≥ 3 t max. GVW. Portugal: no information available.

Sources: DIW, INFRAS, HERRY, NERA.

Table A 7: Specific costs of roads in Europe 1994, in 1000 ECU per km, at 1994 prices - Motorways -

	A[1]	B	DK	SF	F[2]	D	GR	IRL	I	L	NL	P[3]	E	S	CH[4]	UK
Gross capital value per km[5)6)]	n.a.	n.a.	n.a.	n.a.	n.a.	7 076	n.a.	n.a.	n.a.	n.a.	n.a.	n.a.	n.a.	n.a.	n.a.	n.a.
Net capital value per km[5)6)]	5 559	n.a.	n.a.	n.a.	9 040	5 330	n.a.	n.a.	n.a.	n.a.	n.a.	n.a.	n.a.	n.a.	11 027	n.a.
Capital costs per km[7)8)]	177.6	n.a.	n.a.	n.a.	318.7	284.0	n.a.	n.a.	n.a.	n.a.	n.a.	112.9	n.a.	n.a.	1 006.1	n.a.
Running costs per km[9)]	84.8	n.a.	n.a.	n.a.	192.8	71.1	n.a.	n.a.	n.a.	n.a.	n.a.	47.3	n.a.	n.a.	113.9	n.a.
Total infrastructure costs per km	262.4	n.a.	n.a.	n.a.	n.a.	355.1	n.a.	n.a.	n.a.	n.a.	n.a.	160.2	n.a.	n.a.	n.a.	n.a.
Costs of motorised traffic per km	244.6	n.a.	n.a.	n.a.	n.a.	355.1	n.a.	n.a.	n.a.	n.a.	n.a.	160.2	n.a.	n.a.	1 119.9	n.a.
Costs of HGV per km[10)]	102.5	n.a.	n.a.	n.a.	n.a.	219.2	n.a.	n.a.	n.a.	n.a.	n.a.	33.8	n.a.	n.a.	194.5	n.a.

[1] 1990 figures, at 1990 prices. - [2] Net capital value and capital costs are 1995 figures (at 1995 prices). Running costs 1990 (at 1990 prices). - [3] 1995 figures, at 1995 prices. Only motorways run by BRISA. - [4] At current prices. - [5] As at 31 December. Austria: there was no information to which reference day the data refer. - [6] Including land value. - [7] Calculated as average over the year. Austria: there was no information to which reference period the data refer. Switzerland: only costs of road use for transport related functions. - [8] Including land costs. - [9] Switzerland: only costs of road use for transport related functions. - [10] Goods vehicles ≥ 3.5 t max. GVW. Austria: ≥ 4 t max. GVW. Portugal: no information available. Switzerland: ≥ 3 t max. GVW.

Sources: DIW, INFRAS, HERRY, NERA.

Table A 8: Specific costs of roads in Europe 1994, in 1000 ECU (PPP) per km, at 1994 prices - Motorways -

	A[1]	B	DK	SF	F[2]	D	GR	IRL	I	L	NL	P[3]	E	S	CH[4]	UK
Gross capital value per km[5)6)]	n.a.	n.a.	n.a.	n.a.	n.a.	6 274	n.a.	n.a.	n.a.	n.a.	n.a.	n.a.	n.a.	n.a.	n.a.	n.a.
Net capital value per km[5)6)]	5 646	n.a.	n.a.	n.a.	8 804	4 726	n.a.	n.a.	n.a.	n.a.	n.a.	n.a.	n.a.	n.a.	10 139	n.a.
Capital costs per km[7)8)]	180.4	n.a.	n.a.	n.a.	310.4	251.8	n.a.	n.a.	n.a.	n.a.	n.a.	224.0	n.a.	n.a.	925.1	n.a.
Running costs per km[9)]	86.1	n.a.	n.a.	n.a.	197.3	63.0	n.a.	n.a.	n.a.	n.a.	n.a.	93.7	n.a.	n.a.	104.7	n.a.
Total infrastructure costs per km	266.5	n.a.	n.a.	n.a.	n.a.	314.8	n.a.	n.a.	n.a.	n.a.	n.a.	317.7	n.a.	n.a.	n.a.	n.a.
Costs of motorised traffic per km	248.5	n.a.	n.a.	n.a.	n.a.	314.8	n.a.	n.a.	n.a.	n.a.	n.a.	317.7	n.a.	n.a.	1 029.7	n.a.
Costs of HGV per km[10)]	104.1	n.a.	n.a.	n.a.	n.a.	194.4	n.a.	n.a.	n.a.	n.a.	n.a.	67.0	n.a.	n.a.	178.8	n.a.

[1)] 1990 figures, at 1990 prices. - [2)] Net capital value and capital costs are 1995 figures (at 1995 prices). Running costs 1990 (at 1990 prices). - [3)] 1995 figures, at 1995 prices. Only motorways run by BRISA. - [4)] At current prices. - [5)] As at 31 December. Austria: there was no information to which reference day the data refer. Luxembourg: rough estimates. United Kingdom: as at 31 March 1995. - [6)] Including land value. - [7)] Calculated as average over the year. Austria: there was no information to which reference period the data refer. Luxembourg: rough estimates. Switzerland: only costs of road use for transport related functions. United Kingdom: calculated as average over financial year. - [8)] Including land costs. - [9)] Switzerland: only costs of road use for transport related functions. - [10)] Goods vehicles ≥ 3.5 t max. GVW. Austria: ≥ 4 t max. GVW. Portugal: no information available. Switzerland: ≥ 3 t max. GVW.

Sources: DIW, INFRAS, HERRY, NERA.

Table A 9: Average infrastructure costs per vehicle-km for roads in Europe 1994 in ECU per vkm, at 1994 prices - Total road network -

	A[1]	B[2]	DK[2]	SF[3]	F	D	GR	IRL	I	L	NL	P[4]	E[5]	S	CH[6]	UK[7]
All vehicles[8]	**0.044**	**0.025**	**0.033**	**0.036**	**n.a.**	**0.045**	**n.a.**	**0.022**	**n.a.**	**0.036**	**0.037**	**0.009**	**0.037**	**0.035**	**0.075**	**0.025**
Passenger cars[9]	0.021	0.020	0.028	0.021	n.a.	0.026	n.a.	0.019	n.a.	0.030	0.030	0.006	0.031	0.027	0.069	0.021
Buses	0.288	0.056	n.a.	0.083	n.a.	0.128	n.a.	0.038	n.a.	0.083	0.097	0.017	0.045	0.134	0.197	0.042
Light goods vehicles[10][11]	0.103	0.022	n.a.	n.a.	n.a.	0.029	n.a.	0.019	n.a.	0.033	0.033	0.008	0.031	0.028	0.083	0.021
Heavy goods vehicles[12]	0.349	0.073	0.100	0.250	n.a.	0.233	n.a.	0.060	n.a.	0.096	0.131	0.034	0.067	0.144	0.210	0.079
Rigid goods vehicles[13]	0.262	0.054	0.064	n.a.	n.a.	0.195	n.a.	0.040	n.a.	0.077	0.104	n.a.	0.061	0.084	0.156	0.046
Lorries with trailer	n.a.	0.085	0.273	n.a.	n.a.	0.272	n.a.	n.a.	n.a.	0.106	0.161	n.a.	0.083	0.244	0.331	n.a.
Articulated vehicles[14]	0.428	0.085	0.200	n.a.	n.a.	0.253	n.a.	0.101	n.a.	0.123	0.154	n.a.	n.a.	0.228	0.320	0.141

[1] 1990 figures, at 1990 prices. - [2] At current prices. - [3] 1995 figures. Public road network only. 1994 mileages used. - [4] 1995 figures, at 1995 prices. National road network without motorways. - [5] National road network only. - [6] At current prices. - [7] Financial year 1 April 1994 to 31 March 1995. - [8] Belgium, Denmark, Sweden: including motorcycles. Germany: including motorcycles, mopeds, special and agricultural vehicles. Ireland: including special and agricultural vehicles. The Netherlands: including motorcycles, agricultural and special vehicles. Switzerland: including motorcycles and mopeds. - [9] Denmark: passenger cars including motorcycles, buses and light goods vehicles. Portugal: including motorcycles. Switzerland: including motorcycles. Portugal: passenger cars including motorcycles. - [10] Goods vehicles < 3.5 t max. GVW. Austria: < 4 t max. GVW. Denmark, Switzerland: < 3 t max. GVW. Portugal: no information available. - [11] Ireland, Portugal: light goods vehicles including special and agricultural vehicles. - [12] Goods vehicles ≥ 3.5 t max. GVW. Austria: ≥ 4 t max. GVW. Denmark, Switzerland: ≥ 3 t max. GVW. Portugal: no information available. - [13] Austria: rigid goods vehicles including lorries with trailer. - [14] Ireland: articulated vehicles including goods vehicles with trailer.

Sources: DIW, INFRAS, HERRY, NERA.

Table A 10: Average infrastructure costs per vehicle-km for roads in Europe 1994 in ECU (PPP) per vkm, at 1994 prices - Total road network -

	A[1]	B	DK[2]	SF[3]	F	D	GR	IRL	I	L	NL	P[4]	E[5]	S	CH[6]	UK[7]
All vehicles[8]	**0.045**	**0.027**	**0.032**	**0.051**	**n.a.**	**0.040**	**n.a.**	**0.030**	**n.a.**	**0.031**	**0.031**	**0.018**	**0.039**	**0.030**	**0.069**	**0.028**
Passenger cars[9]	0.022	0.021	0.027	0.029	n.a.	0.023	n.a.	0.026	n.a.	0.026	0.026	0.011	0.033	0.022	0.063	0.023
Buses	0.292	0.059	n.a.	0.117	n.a.	0.114	n.a.	0.052	n.a.	0.072	0.082	0.034	0.047	0.112	0.181	0.046
Light goods vehicles[10][11]	0.105	0.023	n.a.	n.a.	n.a.	0.026	n.a.	0.026	n.a.	0.029	0.028	0.015	0.033	0.023	0.076	0.023
Heavy goods vehicles[12]	0.354	0.076	0.097	0.351	n.a.	0.207	n.a.	0.083	n.a.	0.084	0.111	0.067	0.071	0.121	0.193	0.087
Rigid goods vehicles[13]	0.266	0.057	0.061	n.a.	n.a.	0.173	n.a.	0.054	n.a.	0.067	0.088	n.a.	0.064	0.071	0.144	0.050
Lorries with trailer	n.a.	0.089	0.264	n.a.	n.a.	0.242	n.a.	n.a.	n.a.	0.092	0.136	n.a.	0.087	0.205	0.304	n.a.
Articulated vehicles[14]	0.435	0.089	0.193	n.a.	n.a.	0.224	n.a.	0.139	n.a.	0.106	0.131	n.a.	n.a.	0.192	0.295	0.155

1) 1990 figures, at 1990 prices. - 2) At current prices. - 3) 1995 figures. Public road network only. 1994 mileages used. - 4) 1995 figures, at 1995 prices. National road network without motorways. - 5) National road network only. - 6) At current prices. - 7) Financial year 1 April 1994 to 31 March 1995. - 8) Belgium, Denmark, Sweden: including motorcycles. Germany: including motorcycles, mopeds, special and agricultural vehicles. Ireland: including special and agricultural vehicles. The Netherlands: including motorcycles and special vehicles. Portugal: including motorcycles, agricultural and special vehicles. Switzerland: including motorcycles and mopeds. - 9) Denmark: passenger cars including motorcycles, buses and light goods vehicles. Portugal: passenger cars including motorcycles. - 10) Goods vehicles < 3.5 t max. GVW. Austria: < 4 t max. GVW. Denmark, Switzerland: < 3 t max. GVW. Portugal: no information available. - 11) Ireland, Portugal: light goods vehicles including special and agricultural vehicles. - 12) Goods vehicles ≥ 3.5 t max. GVW. Austria: ≥ 4 t max. GVW. Denmark, Switzerland: ≥ 3 t max. GVW. Portugal: no information available. - 13) Austria: rigid goods vehicles including lorries with trailer. - 14) Ireland: articulated vehicles including goods vehicles with trailer.

Sources: DIW, INFRAS, HERRY, NERA.

Table A 11: Average infrastructure costs per vehicle-km for roads in Europe 1994 in ECU per vkm, at 1994 prices - Motorways -

	A[1]	B	DK	SF	F	D	GR	IRL	I	L	NL	P[2]	E	S	CH[3]	UK
All vehicles[4]	**0.030**	**n.a.**	**n.a.**	**n.a.**	**n.a.**	**0.022**	**n.a.**	**n.a.**	**n.a.**	**n.a.**	**n.a.**	**0.016**	**n.a.**	**n.a.**	**0.096**	**n.a.**
Passenger cars	0.016	n.a.	n.a.	n.a.	n.a.	0.009	n.a.	n.a.	n.a.	n.a.	n.a.	0.012	n.a.	n.a.	0.086	n.a.
Buses	0.128	n.a.	n.a.	n.a.	n.a.	0.083	n.a.	n.a.	n.a.	n.a.	n.a.	0.065	n.a.	n.a.	0.184	n.a.
Light goods vehicles[5]	0.075	n.a.	n.a.	n.a.	n.a.	0.127	n.a.	n.a.	n.a.	n.a.	n.a.	0.021	n.a.	n.a.	0.105	n.a.
Heavy goods vehicles[6]	0.140	n.a.	n.a.	n.a.	n.a.	0.091	n.a.	n.a.	n.a.	n.a.	n.a.	0.079	n.a.	n.a.	0.260	n.a.
Rigid goods vehicles[7]	0.098	n.a.	n.a.	n.a.	n.a.	0.108	n.a.	n.a.	n.a.	n.a.	n.a.	n.a.	n.a.	n.a.	0.179	n.a.
Lorries with trailer	n.a.	n.a.	n.a.	n.a.	n.a.	0.093	n.a.	n.a.	n.a.	n.a.	n.a.	n.a.	n.a.	n.a.	0.395	n.a.
Articulated vehicles	0.167	n.a.	n.a.	n.a.	n.a.	0.074	n.a.	n.a.	n.a.	n.a.	n.a.	n.a.	n.a.	n.a.	0.801	n.a.

[1] 1990 figures, at 1990 prices. - [2] 1995 figures, at 1995 prices. Only motorways run by BRISA. - [3] At current prices. - [4] Austria: including motorcycles. Germany: including motorcycles, mopeds, special and agricultural vehicles. Switzerland: including motorcycles and mopeds. - [5] Goods vehicles < 3.5 t max. GVW. Austria: < 4 t max. GVW. Portugal: no information available. Switzerland: < 3 t max. GVW. - [6] Goods vehicles ≥ 3.5 t max. GVW. Austria: ≥ 4 t max. GVW. Portugal: no information available. Switzerland: ≥ 3 t max. GVW. - [7] Austria: rigid goods vehicles including lorries with trailer.

Sources: DIW, INFRAS, HERRY, NERA.

Table A 12: Average infrastructure costs per vehicle-km for roads in Europe 1994 in ECU (PPP) per vkm, at 1994 prices - Motorways -

	A[1]	B	DK	SF	F	D	GR	IRL	I	L	NL	P[2]	E	S	CH[3]	UK
All vehicles[4]	**0.031**	**n.a.**	**n.a.**	**n.a.**	**n.a.**	**0.020**	**n.a.**	**n.a.**	**n.a.**	**n.a.**	**n.a.**	**0.032**	**n.a.**	**n.a.**	**0.089**	**n.a.**
Passenger cars	0.016	n.a.	n.a.	n.a.	n.a.	0.008	n.a.	n.a.	n.a.	n.a.	n.a.	0.023	n.a.	n.a.	0.079	n.a.
Buses	0.130	n.a.	n.a.	n.a.	n.a.	0.074	n.a.	n.a.	n.a.	n.a.	n.a.	0.128	n.a.	n.a.	0.169	n.a.
Light goods vehicles[5]	0.076	n.a.	n.a.	n.a.	n.a.	0.112	n.a.	n.a.	n.a.	n.a.	n.a.	0.041	n.a.	n.a.	0.097	n.a.
Heavy goods vehicles[6]	0.142	n.a.	n.a.	n.a.	n.a.	0.081	n.a.	n.a.	n.a.	n.a.	n.a.	0.156	n.a.	n.a.	0.239	n.a.
Rigid goods vehicles[7]	0.100	n.a.	n.a.	n.a.	n.a.	0.095	n.a.	n.a.	n.a.	n.a.	n.a.	n.a.	n.a.	n.a.	0.164	n.a.
Lorries with trailer	n.a.	n.a.	n.a.	n.a.	n.a.	0.082	n.a.	n.a.	n.a.	n.a.	n.a.	n.a.	n.a.	n.a.	0.363	n.a.
Articulated vehicles	0.169	n.a.	n.a.	n.a.	n.a.	0.066	n.a.	n.a.	n.a.	n.a.	n.a.	n.a.	n.a.	n.a.	0.737	n.a.

[1] 1990 figures, at 1990 prices. - [2] 1995 figures, at 1995 prices. Only motorways run by BRISA. - [3] At current prices. - [4] Austria: including motorcycles. Germany: including motorcycles, mopeds, special and agricultural vehicles. Switzerland: including motorcycles and mopeds. - [5] Goods vehicles < 3.5 t max. GVW. Austria: < 4 t max. GVW. Portugal: no information available. Switzerland: < 3 t max. GVW. - [6] Goods vehicles ≥ 3.5 t max. GVW. Austria: ≥ 4 t max. GVW. Portugal: no information available. Switzerland: ≥ 3 t max. GVW. - [7] Austria: rigid goods vehicles including lorries with trailer.

Sources: DIW, INFRAS, HERRY, NERA.

Table A 13: Marginal infrastructure costs per vehicle-km for roads in Europe 1994 in ECU per vkm, at 1994 prices - Total road network -

	A	B	DK[1]	SF[2]	F[3]	D	GR	IRL	I	L	NL	P[4]	E[5]	S	CH[6]	UK[7]
All vehicles[8]	**n.a.**	**n.a.**	**n.a.**	**0.0022**	**0.0077**	**0.0073**	**n.a.**	**0.0029**	**n.a.**	**n.a.**	**n.a.**	**n.a.**	**0.0027**	**0.0037**	**n.a.**	**0.0034**
Passenger cars	n.a.	n.a.	n.a.	0.0011	0.0043	-	n.a.	0.0010	n.a.	n.a.	n.a.	n.a.	0.0002	0.0013	n.a.	0.0005
Buses	n.a.	n.a.	n.a.	0.0046	0.0273	0.0495	n.a.	0.0117	n.a.	n.a.	n.a.	n.a.	0.0024	0.0325	n.a.	0.0108
Light goods vehicles[9] [10]	n.a.	n.a.	n.a.	n.a.	0.0070	0.0002	n.a.	0.0010	n.a.	n.a.	n.a.	n.a.	0.0002	0.0016	n.a.	0.0005
Heavy goods vehicles[11]	n.a.	n.a.	0.0452	0.0173	0.0565	0.0857	n.a.	0.0302	n.a.	n.a.	n.a.	0.0186	0.0167	0.0310	0.358	0.0408
Rigid trucks	n.a.	n.a.	0.0060	n.a.	0.0503	0.0796	n.a.	0.0131	n.a.	n.a.	n.a.	n.a.	0.0161	0.0146	0.339	0.0139
Trucks with trailer	n.a.	n.a.	0.1989	n.a.	0.0496	0.0870	n.a.	n.a.	n.a.	n.a.	n.a.	n.a.	0.0180	0.0580	0.401	n.a.
Articulated vehicles[12]	n.a.	n.a.	0.1741	n.a.	0.0621	0.0952	n.a.	0.0637	n.a.	n.a.	n.a.	n.a.	n.a.	0.0547	0.370	0.0902

[1] At current prices. - [2] 1995 figures. Public road network only. 1994 mileages used. - [3] 1990 figures, at 1990 prices. - [4] 1995 figure, at 1995 prices. National road network without motorways. - [5] National road network only. - [6] Marginal infrastructure costs: 60 % of maintenance, 50 % of running costs. At current prices. - [7] Financial year 1 April 1994 to 31 March 1995. - [8] Germany: including motorcycles, mopeds, special and agricultural vehicles. Ireland: including special and agricultural vehicles. Sweden: including motorcycles. - [9] Goods vehicles < 3.5 t max. GVW. - [10] Ireland: light goods vehicles including special and agricultural vehicles. - [11] Goods vehicles ≥ 3.5 t max. GVW. Denmark, Switzerland: ≥ 3 t max. GVW. Portugal: no information available. - [12] Ireland: articulated vehicles including goods vehicles with trailer.

Sources: DIW, INFRAS, HERRY, NERA.

Table A 14: Marginal infrastructure costs per vehicle-km for roads in Europe 1994 in ECU (PPP) per vkm, at 1994 prices - Total road network -

	A	B	DK[1]	SF[2]	F[3]	D	GR	IRL	I	L	NL	P[4]	E[5]	S	CH[6]	UK[7]
All vehicles[8]	**n.a.,**	**n.a.**	**n.a.**	**0.0030**	**0.0083**	**0.0065**	**n.a.**	**0.0040**	**n.a.**	**n.a.**	**n.a.**	**n.a.**	**0.0028**	**0.0031**	**n.a.**	**0.0038**
Passenger cars	n.a.	n.a.	n.a.	0.0015	0.0046	-	n.a.	0.0014	n.a.	n.a.	n.a.	n.a.	0.0002	0.0011	n.a.	0.0004
Buses	n.a.	n.a.	n.a.	0.0065	0.0296	0.0439	n.a.	0.0159	n.a.	n.a.	n.a.	n.a.	0.0025	0.0273	n.a.	0.0119
Light goods vehicles[9][10]	n.a.	n.a.	n.a.	n.a.	0.0076	0.0002	n.a.	0.0014	n.a.	n.a.	n.a.	n.a.	0.0002	0.0013	n.a.	0.0004
Heavy goods vehicles[11]	n.a.	n.a.	0.0437	0.0242	0.0613	0.0760	n.a.	0.0413	n.a.	n.a.	n.a.	0.0368	0.0174	0.0260	0.329	0.0450
Rigid trucks	n.a.	n.a.	0.0058	n.a.	0.0545	0.0706	n.a.	0.0179	n.a.	n.a.	n.a.	n.a.	0.0169	0.0123	0.312	0.0153
Trucks with trailer	n.a.	n.a.	0.1921	n.a.	0.0538	0.0771	n.a.	n.a.	n.a.	n.a.	n.a.	n.a.	0.0188	0.0488	0.369	n.a.
Articulated vehicles[12]	n.a.	n.a.	0.1681	n.a.	0.0673	0.0844	n.a.	0.0873	n.a.	n.a.	n.a.	n.a.	n.a.	0.0460	0.340	0.0994

[1] At current prices. - [2] 1995 figures. - [3] 1990 figures, at 1990 prices. - [4] 1995 figure, at 1995 prices. National road network without motorways. - [5] National road network only. - [6] Marginal infrastructure costs: 60 % of maintenance, 50 % of running costs. At current prices. - [7] Financial year 1 April 1994 to 31 March 1995. - [8] Germany: including motorcycles, mopeds, special and agricultural vehicles. Ireland: including special and agricultural vehicles. Sweden: including motorcycles. - [9] Goods vehicles < 3.5 t max. GVW. - [10] Ireland: light goods vehicles including special and agricultural vehicles. - [11] Goods vehicles ≥ 3.5 t max. GVW. Denmark, Switzerland: ≥ 3 t max. GVW. Portugal: no information available. - [12] Ireland: articulated vehicles including goods vehicles with trailer.

Sources: DIW, INFRAS, HERRY, NERA.

Table A 15. Marginal infrastructure costs per vehicle-km for roads in Europe 1994 in ECU per vkm, at 1994 prices - Motorways -

	A	B	DK	SF	F[1]	D	GR	IRL	I	L	NL	P[2]	E	S	CH[3]	UK
All vehicles[4]	**n.a.**	**n.a.**	**n.a.**	**n.a.**	**0.0113**	**0.0036**	**n.a.**	**n.a.**	**n.a.**	**n.a.**	**n.a.**	**n.a.**	**n.a.**	**n.a.**	**n.a.**	**n.a.**
Passenger cars	n.a.	n.a.	n.a.	n.a.	0.0072	-	n.a.	n.a.	n.a.	n.a.	n.a.	n.a.	n.a.	n.a.	n.a.	n.a.
Buses	n.a.	n.a.	n.a.	n.a.	0.0159	0.0574	n.a.	n.a.	n.a.	n.a.	n.a.	n.a.	n.a.	n.a.	n.a.	n.a.
Light goods vehicles[5]	n.a.	n.a.	n.a.	n.a.	0.0087	0.0000	n.a.	n.a.	n.a.	n.a.	n.a.	n.a.	n.a.	n.a.	n.a.	n.a.
Heavy goods vehicles[6]	n.a.	n.a.	n.a.	n.a.	0.0334	0.0212	n.a.	n.a.	n.a.	n.a.	n.a.	0.0496	n.a.	n.a.	0.173	n.a.
Rigid goods vehicles	n.a.	n.a.	n.a.	n.a.	0.0277	0.0157	n.a.	n.a.	n.a.	n.a.	n.a.	n.a.	n.a.	n.a.	0.160	n.a.
Lorries with trailer	n.a.	n.a.	n.a.	n.a.	0.0261	0.0256	n.a.	n.a.	n.a.	n.a.	n.a.	n.a.	n.a.	n.a.	0.191	n.a.
Articulated vehicles	n.a.	n.a.	n.a.	n.a.	0.0364	0.0225	n.a.	n.a.	n.a.	n.a.	n.a.	n.a.	n.a.	n.a.	0.191	n.a.

[1] 1990 figures, at 1990 prices. - [2] 1995 figure, at 1995 prices. Only motorways run by BRISA. - [3] Marginal costs: 60 % of maintenance, 50 % of running costs. At current prices. - [4] Germany: including motorcycles, mopeds, special and agricultural vehicles. - [5] Goods vehicles ≥ 3.5 t max. GVW. Portugal: no information available. Switzerland: ≥ 3 t max. GVW. - [6] Goods vehicles < 3.5 t max. GVW. GVW. - [6] Goods

Sources: DIW, INFRAS, HERRY, NERA.

Table A 16. Marginal infrastructure costs per vehicle-km for roads in Europe 1994 in ECU (PPP) per vkm, at 1994 prices - Motorways -

	A	B	DK	SF	F[1]	D	GR	IRL	I	L	NL	P[2]	E	S	CH[3]	UK
All vehicles[4]	**n.a.**	**n.a.**	**n.a.**	**n.a.**	**0.0123**	**0.0032**	**n.a.**	**n.a.**	**n.a.**	**n.a.**	**n.a.**	**n.a.**	**n.a.**	**n.a.**	**n.a.**	**n.a.**
Passenger cars	n.a.	n.a.	n.a.	n.a.	0.0078	-	n.a.	n.a.	n.a.	n.a.	n.a.	n.a.	n.a.	n.a.	n.a.	n.a.
Buses	n.a.	n.a.	n.a.	n.a.	0.0173	0.0509	n.a.	n.a.	n.a.	n.a.	n.a.	n.a.	n.a.	n.a.	n.a.	n.a.
Light goods vehicles[5]	n.a.	n.a.	n.a.	n.a.	0.0094	0.0000	n.a.	n.a.	n.a.	n.a.	n.a.	n.a.	n.a.	n.a.	n.a.	n.a.
Heavy goods vehicles[6]	n.a.	n.a.	n.a.	n.a.	0.0363	0.0188	n.a.	n.a.	n.a.	n.a.	n.a.	0.0983	n.a.	n.a.	0.159	n.a.
Rigid goods vehicles	n.a.	n.a.	n.a.	n.a.	0.0301	0.0139	n.a.	n.a.	n.a.	n.a.	n.a.	n.a.	n.a.	n.a.	0.147	n.a.
Lorries with trailer	n.a.	n.a.	n.a.	n.a.	0.0283	0.0227	n.a.	n.a.	n.a.	n.a.	n.a.	n.a.	n.a.	n.a.	0.176	n.a.
Articulated vehicles	n.a.	n.a.	n.a.	n.a.	0.0395	0.0199	n.a.	n.a.	n.a.	n.a.	n.a.	n.a.	n.a.	n.a.	0.176	n.a.

[1] 1990 figures, at 1990 prices. - [2] 1995 figure, at 1995 prices. Only motorways run by BRISA. - [3] Marginal costs: 60 % of maintenance, 50 % of running costs. At current prices. - [4] Germany: including motorcycles, mopeds, special and agricultural vehicles. - [5] Goods vehicles ≥ 3.5 t max. GVW. - [6] Goods vehicles < 3.5 t max. GVW. Portugal: no information available. Switzerland: ≥ 3 t max. GVW.

Sources: DIW, INFRAS, HERRY, NERA.

Table A 17: Input data for the congestion cost model: time values per hour and national fuel prices 1994

Country	Time values per hour in ECU		Source of information	Fuel prices in ECU/litre [1]	
	Value per car	Value per goods vehicle		Petrol	Diesel
Austria	14.7	29.5	Schierhaekl, K. and Glaser, S. (1995): Analysis of average traffic flow and road capacity. Study commissioned by ÖAMTC.	0.752	0.486
Belgium	7.8	29.7	Mayeres, I., Ochelen, S. and Proost, S. (1996): The marginal external costs of urban transport. Transportation Research D, 1D, 111-130.	0.774	0.515
Denmark	7.2	20.9	Ministry of Transport (1992): Danish highway investment evaluation model. Updated.	0.413	0.409
Finland	4.9	6.0	Pursula, M. and Kurri, J. "Value of time research in Finland", Helsinki University of Technology Transportation Engineering (figures from Finnish National Roads Authority).	0.736	0.487
France	11.2	29.3	Service d'Etudes Techniques des Routes at Autoroutes (SETRA).	0.800	0.494
Germany	4.6	28.3	FGSV (1997): Kommentar zum Entwurf "Empfehlungen für Wirtschaftlichkeitsuntersuchungen an Straßen" (EWS), Aktualisierung des RAS-W '86. Köln.	0.809	0.516
Greece	6.4	7.9	Car figures from Pursula, M. (1997): The transprice trans-European car driver VOT survey, Helsinki University of Technology Transportation Engineering, Seminar Paper. Goods vehicles calculated using UK ratios. (Athens only)	0.651	0.383
Ireland	11.3	13.9	National Roads Authority, Dublin.	0.702	0.568
Italy	10.9	13.3	Car figures from Pursula, M. (1997): The transprice trans-European car driver VOT survey, Helsinki University of Technology Transportation Engineering, Seminar Paper. Goods vehicles calculated using UK ratios. (Como only)	0.825	0.543
Luxembourg	13.5	16.5	These figures were estimated using UK ratios of values of time to average hourly earnings of manual workers, applied to national average manual wage rates for 1994-95, and adjusted for inflation.	0.600	0.439
Netherlands	7.8	9.6	Hague Consulting Group (1990): The Netherlands Value of Time Study. The Hague.	0.878	0.617
Portugal	4.3	5.2	These figures were estimated using UK ratios of values of time to average hourly earnings of manual workers, applied to national average manual wage rates for 1994-95, and adjusted for inflation.	0.768	0.502
Spain	9.9	16.4	Ministerio de Fomento, Carreteras Planificacion Recomendaciones, Para la Evaluacion Economica, Coste-Beneficio des Estudios y Proyectos de Carreteras.	0.664	0.445
Sweden	5.4	21.5	SAMPLAN (1995): Översyn av samhällsekonomiska kallkyvärden för den nationella trafikplaneringen 1994-1998, Stockholm.	0.819	0.547
Switzerland	27.2	61.5	INFRAS (1997): Congestion costs in Switzerland. Interim report, Department of Transport and communication.	0.813	0.651
United Kingdom	9.9	12.2	Department of Transport (UK), Design manual for roads and bridges, Vol. 13, economic evaluation of road schemes, section 1, The COBA Manual, Section 2, Highways Economics, note 2.	0.663	0.565

1) Source: International Energy Agency (1998): Energy Prices and Taxes, third quarter 1997, OECD/IEA.

Annex B - Glossary

AASH(T)O factors

Factors which describe the impacts between axle-load and road deformation. The AASH(T)O factors were yielded by the AASHO road test carried out in the US in 1958 in Illinois. The result of this test was that the road deformation increases with the fourth power of axle-load (4th power rule).

Annuity method

A financial-mathematical method for calculating the annual refinancing of investments. The annuities are calculated by using the formula:

$$a = u \cdot \frac{\dfrac{z}{100} \cdot \left(1 + \dfrac{z}{100}\right)^{d}}{\left(1 + \dfrac{z}{100}\right)^{d} - 1}$$

with:

a	annuity for the capital value
u	capital value
z	interest rate in percent
d	depreciation period (years) for the road assets

In economic terms, the annuity value a is equal to the annual sum which, when discounted over the life of the asset (i. e. the depreciation period d) has a present value equal to that of the capital value u.

Articulated vehicles

Articulated vehicles are goods vehicle combinations consisting of a tractor with a semi-trailer whereby only the semi-trailer carries the payload.

Average costs

Average costs are equal to the total costs of roads divided by a measure of output, such as vehicle-kms. They therefore show the costs of road provision per unit of traffic. They are particularly relevant for cost-recovery, since prices which are set equal to average costs will ensure that total costs are recovered from users. Average costs contain both fixed and variable costs. Due to this fact, they are usually calculated in order to get information on total road costs and - in combination with revenues - on cost recovery.

Axle weight-km

One of the factors used for allocating weight dependent costs to vehicle types. They are obtained by multiplying the weight in tons on each axle with the mileage driven. The weight in tons on each axle can be derived either from the maximum gross vehicle weight or from the average gross vehicle weight.

Capacity costs

Capacity costs are those costs which occur due to the provision of road capacity independently of the level of traffic. They comprise shares of capital costs and running costs and are equal to the fixed costs.

Capital costs

The capital costs comprise the consumption of fixed capital ($\rightarrow$ depreciation) and the interest ($\rightarrow$ interest). Capital costs represent a high share of total road costs and are different to the annual capital expenditures.

Capital value

The capital value is the value of fixed capital measured either as a gross or a net value. The *gross value* represents the capital value of all assets still physically existing in the capital stock. It can thus be considered as an equivalent of production capacity. The *net value* represents the value of assets minus the meanwhile consumed fixed capital ($\rightarrow$ depreciation). The difference to the gross value is thus the loss of value due to foreseen obsolence and the normal amount of accidential damage which is not made good by normal repair, as well as normal wear and tear. Methods for estimating capital values are the direct method ($\rightarrow$ synthetic method) and the indirect method ($\rightarrow$ perpetual inventory concept).

Congestion

Congestion arises when traffic exceeds road capacity so that the speed of vehicles is slowed down. It can be defined as a situation where traffic is slower than it would be if traffic flows were at low levels. The definition of these „low levels" (reference level) is complicated and varies from country to country (e.g. six service levels in the American HCM).

Congestion costs

Congestion costs are costs which vehicles suffer because they are slowed down by other vehicles (suffering approach). They can comprise direct costs (time costs, operating costs) and indirect costs (opportunity costs for the time loss, costs occurred to third parties due to delayed deliveries of goods, environmental costs). In this study congestion costs are defined as the difference between the total costs of travel of existing traffic flows and the costs of travel for a reference flow-level.

Cost approach

There are two principal ways for elaborating road accounts: the cost-based approach and the expenditure-based approach. The cost approach is based on deriving capital cost from existing road capital values. This implies that investments with an expected lifetime of more than one year have to be capitalised (that means depreciation and interests have to be calculated).

Cost coverage

Cost coverage is the ratio between revenues and costs. It answers the question whether the costs are covered by the (respective) revenues.

Depreciation

Depreciation is an accounting charge for the decline in value of an asset spread over its economic life (life expectancy). The depreciation is a part of deriving capital costs from existing road capital values. In general there are two approaches to derive capital costs: (1) The perpetual inventory method: (2) The annuity method (see annuity-method).

Expenditures

The annually spent money for roads. They contain investments (comprising net-investments for the construction of new roads and for enlargement as well as replacement investments) and running expenditure for road maintenance, road operation and administration/police.

Expenditure approach

One of the two principal ways for elaborating road accounts. It is based on using (annual) expenditures for investment, maintenance and operation. In this approach the annual investment expenditures are not capitalised.

External costs

External costs (of infrastructure) are uncovered infrastructure costs. That means, external costs are those costs which the (infrastructure) user does not pay for.

Fixed costs

Fixed costs are equal to those costs, which are independent on the (vehicle) mileage driven.

GVW

GVW is the gross vehicle weight and contains the weight of the vehicle itself and the weight of the payload.

HGV

HGV means heavy goods vehicles. Within this study they are defined as all goods vehicles with a maximum GVW equal or more than 3,5 tons.

Internal costs

Internal costs (of infrastructure) are those infrastructure costs which the (infrastructure) user pays for.

Interest

Interest charges are part of the capital costs of road infrastructure. They refelect the opportunity cost of capital (if not invested in roads the funds could be invested elsewhere in the economy). The interest rate for road infrastructure capital is usually comparable with the refinancing cost for governmental loans. The estimation of capital charges with a nominal interest rate (i.e. including a premium for inflation) is necessary if the capital value does not consider inflation rates (e.g. is calculated by the use of nominal investment costs = purchase costs).

A real interest rate has to be used, if the capital values have been calculated at current prices.

Investment expenditures

They reflect the annual expenditures for road infrastructure with durable character and a lifetime of more than one year (for example new construction of roads or reconstruction of road surface). These expenditures have to be capitalised with a depreciation rate and an interest rate reflecting the opportunity cost for the capital invested.

Load capacity

Carrying capacity (passenger, tons) of a vehicle. A 40 tonne truck for example has a load capacity of around 30 tonnes. See also: payload.

Lost assets

These are assets which are already amortised (e.g. which have exceeded their expected lifetime).

Maintenance

Maintenance costs reflect the costs which are necessary to maintain an existing infrastructure. We distinguish between

– ordinary maintenance, for example cleaning and winter maintenance, which is independent of road use and

– maintenance, which is dependent of the volume of vehicles or vkm (e.g. surface dressing). These latter maintenance costs are variable cost and weight dependent.

Marginal costs - short term

Marginal costs are specific variable costs, referring on the mileage driven on existing infrastructure (without considering a capacity increase). They reflect the additional costs of an additional vehicle or vkm. Regarding infrastructure these costs are mainly weight dependent maintenance costs (see → maintenance).

Marginal costs - long term

Additionally to short term marginal infrastructure costs, long term marginal costs do consider possible new investments or capacity increases. The calculation of these cost is rather difficult since it has to be known which future infrastructure are necessary and appropriate. To find an optimal path for capacity increases, an infrastructure operator has to compare marginal congestion costs and marginal investment costs for future capacity increases.

Operating expenditures

These are expenditures which are necessary to operate an existing road network (administration, police, traffic signals, cleaning). These costs are running costs and thus do not have to be capitalised.

Payload

The weight of the freight carried by a goods vehicle. The payload will be equal or less than the carrying capacity.

Perpetual-inventory method

This is a method to estimate the capital value from a time series of annual investment expenditures. Annual new investments are cumulated and - according to their remaining life time - a depreciation will be calcualated. The sum of these annual remaining capital values is equal to the total amount of the road capital value. (See further details in section 3.3.2 of the study).

PCU (Passenger Car Unit)

PCU is used in order to standardise vehicles in relation to a passenger car. Speed and lengths differentials are most common.

PPP

PPP means purchasing power parity. PPPs are the rates of currency conversions which equalise the purchasing power of different countries. This means that a given sum of money, when converted into different currencies at the PPP rates, will buy the same basket of goods and services in all countries. In particular, PPPs are applied if figures for specific products or branches shall be expressed in foreign currency (for example in ECU or in US $) because in these cases the use of official exchange rates is not appropriate.

Purchase costs

The costs of buying a good or service.

Rigid goods vehicle

A goods vehicle which has a one-piece, rigid, chassis, with two or more axles. Rigid goods vehicles may be able to tow a separate trailer.

Replacement value/cost

The cost of replacing a particular asset of a particular quality with an asset of equivalent quality. Replacement cost may exceed the original purchase cost because of changes in the prices of the assets.

Running expenditures

The costs necessary to keep a particular asset in operation, but which do not enhance the value of the asset. For roads, running expenditures will be those annual expenditures necessary to ensure that roads provide an acceptable quality of service, but which do not maintain that quality beyond a limited period of time. They include items such as: sweeping and cleaning; cutting of grass verges; winter maintenance (snow clearing and gritting); street lighting; and policing.

Running costs

These are equal to running expenditures.

SNA

SNA stands for System of National Accounts, an international framework of definitions and methods for quantifying macroeconomic processes. Nucleus of SNA are the rules for the sector-specific accounts, the tables on production and consumption of GDP and the distributional issues of national income, the gross fixed capital formation by sectors and the input-output tables.

Speed-flow function

A mathematical or graphical relationship between the traffic flow on a particular road, and the speed of that traffic flow. As traffic flows increase, traffic speeds eventually fall.

Standard axle-km

Standard axle-km belong to the weight dependent factors used in cost allocation procedures. They are obtained by multiplying the mileage driven by a certain vehicle type with the standard axle. The standard axle is a measure of the relative road wear and is equal to the sum of the fourth power of the weight in tons on each axle, divided by 10 000 (see also AASH(T)O factors).

Structural maintenance

Maintenance of a capital nature. A good example of structural maintenance is the reconstruction of road pavements and resurfacing. The benefits of this expenditure are received over a number of years, rather than just in the year in which the road pavement is improved.

Survival function

Survival functions are used in rather refined perpetual inventory models. The survival function g (i) is based on the assumption that the service lives of assets within an investment vintage are dispersed around the mean. g (i) explains then which share of investments within an investment-vintage still exists in the capital stock after i years. The survival function is characterised by a downwards slope of shares between 100 % (in the first year of investment) and 0 % (after exceeding the maximal lifetime of all assets in the investment vintage).

Synthetic method

One of the two main methods to value the existing road network (see also: perpetual inventory method). The synthetic method values the road network by estimating what it would cost to replace the road network with assets of equivalent quality. The method therefore involves measuring the existing physical assets, in terms of road length of particular types, bridges, etc, and then multiplying these measures of physical assets by unit replacement costs, such as the cost of constructing a motorway with the same physical characteristics as the existing one.

Total costs

The sum of capital costs and running costs. Total costs therefore give the total annual costs of providing the road network.

Variable costs

Those costs which vary with traffic levels. Examples of variable costs include wear-and-tear to road surfaces (caused largely by the passage of heavy vehicles), and congestion costs.

Vehicle length-km

They belong to the factors used for allocating capacity costs in cost allocation procedures. They are yielded by multiplying the vehicle length of a certain vehicle category with the mileage driven by this category.

List of abbreviations

A	Austria (Österreich)
B	Belgium (België/Belgique)
CH	Switzerland (Schweiz/Suisse)
D	Germany (Deutschland)
DK	Denmark (Danmark)
E	Spain (España)
F	France (France)
GR	Greece (Hellas)
GVW	Gross vehicle weight
HCM	Highway capacity manual
HGV	Heavy goods vehicles
I	Italy (Italia)
IRL	Ireland (Eire/Ireland)
L	Luxembourg (Luxembourg)
LOS	Level of service
NL	Netherlands (Nederlands)

P	Portugal (Portugal)
PCU	Passenger car unit
PPP	Purchasing power parity
S	Sweden (Sverige)
SF	Finland (Suomi Finland)
SNA	System of national accounts
UK	United Kingdom (United Kingdom)
VAT	Value added tax
vkm	vehicle-km

List of tables

List of figures

Literature

Aberle, G. and Holocher, K.H. (1984): Vergleichende Wegerechnungen und Verkehrsinfrastrukturpolitik, Gutachten im Auftrag des Verbandes der Automobilindustrie e.V. *Schriftenreihe des Verbandes der Automobilindustrie e.V. (VDA)*, Nr. 46, Frankfurt am Main.

Arbeitsgruppe Wegekosten im Bundesverkehrsministerium (1969): Bericht über die Kosten der Wege des Eisenbahn-, Straßen- und Binnenschiffsverkehrs in der Bundesrepublik Deutschland. *Schriftenreihe des Bundesministeriums für Verkehr*, Heft 34, Bad Godesberg.

Azienda Nazionale Autonoma delle Strade (1987): Rapporto Concusivo della Commissione Istituita ai sensi della Legge 12 Agosto 1982 n. 553 del 13 Maggio 1986 per lo Studio della Revisione e la Ristrutturazione des Sistema delle Tariffe di Pedaggio Autostradali, Roma.

BFS (Bundesamt für Statistik) (1985): Bericht über die Neugestaltung der Strassenrechnung. Bericht der interdepartementalen Arbeitsgruppe für die Neugestaltung der Strassenrechnung, Bern.

BFS (Bundesamt für Statistik) (1997): Statistisches Jahrbuch der Schweiz.

BMV/DIW (1997): Verkehr in Zahlen 1997, Berlin/Köln.

Brossier, M.C. (1996): Mise à jour du rapport n° 91 - 105 relatif à la nouvelle étude de l'imputation des coûts d'infrastructure de transport routiers.

Cantos, P., Pereira, R., Kiosseoglou, A., and Poveda, J. (1995): The allocation and charging of interurban road infrastructure in Spain. *Financing Transport Infrastructure*. Proceedings of Seminar L held at the PTRC European Transport Forum.

CBS (1997): Kerncijers Verkeer en Vervoer.

Centrum voor energiebesparing en schone technologie (1992): Transport, Economy & Environment, Delft.

Centrum voor energiebesparing en schone technologie (1993): The art of internalizing, Delft.

COWI (1989): Subsidiering i Trafiksektoren 1989, Kopenhagen.

COWI (1994): Subsidiering af Godstransport 1994, Kopenhagen.

Department of Economic and Social Affairs - Statistical Office of the United Nations (1968): A System of National Accounts. *Studies in Methods.* Series F, No. 2, Rev. 3, New York.

Department of Economic and Social Affairs - Statistical Office of the United Nations (1977): Provisonal International Guidelines on the National and Sectoral Balance-sheet and Reconciliation Accounts of the System of National Accounts. *Statistical Papers.* Series M, No. 60, New York.

Department of the Environment (1993): Irish Bulletin of Vehicle and Driver Statistics.

Department of Transport (1996): Design Manual for Roads and Bridges, Volume 13 Economic Assessment of Road Schemes, Section 1 The COBA Manual, Section 2 Highway Economics Note 2.

Department of Transport (1997): Transport Statistics Report: Transport of Goods by Road in Great Britain 1996. The Stationery Office, London (annual publication).

DHV/Tebodin (1992): Kosten op het spoor - Kosten infrastructuur ns-goederenvervoer: Een afleiding op basis van concurrerende vervoerwijzen. On behalf of Ministerie van Verkeer en Waterstaat - Directoraat-General voor het Vervoer, Amersfort/Den Haag.

Dienst GVF EVED (Department of Transport) (1997): Fahrleistungen des privaten Strassenverkehrs 1990-2015, Bern.

DIW (1977): Direkte und indirekte gesamtwirtschaftliche Auswirkungen von Kostenänderungen durch verkehrspolitische Maßnahmen auf Preise, Produktion und Beschäftigung. Gutachten im Auftrag des Bundesministeriums für Verkehr, Berlin.

DIW (1978): Neuberechnung der Wegekosten im Verkehr für das Jahr 1975. *Sonderhefte des DIW,* Nr. 127, Berlin.

DIW (1980): Neuberechnung der Kosten für die Wege des Eisenbahn-, Straßen-, Binnenschiffs- und Luftverkehrs in der Bundesrepublik Deutschland für das Jahr 1978. Gutachten im Auftrag des Bundesministeriums für Verkehr, Berlin.

DIW (1983): Berechnung der Kosten für die Wege des Eisenbahn-, Straßen-, Binnenschiffs- und Luftverkehrs in der Bundesrepublik Deutschland für das Jahr 1981. *Sonderhefte des DIW,* Nr. 137, Berlin.

DIW (1987): Erweiterung methodischer Ansätze zur Wegekostenrechnung und Erarbeitung eines Konzeptes für eine Gesamtkostenrechnung des Verkehrs. Gutachten im Auftrage des Bundesministeriums für Verkehr, Berlin.

DIW (1990): Berechnung der Kosten und der Ausgaben für die Wege des Eisenbahn-, Straßen-, Binnenschiffs- und Luftverkehrs in der Bundesrepublik Deutschland für das Jahr 1987. *Beiträge zur Strukturforschung des DIW,* Heft 119, Berlin.

DIW (1992): Berechnung der Wegekosten- und Wegeausgabendeckungsgrade für den Straßenverkehr in den alten Ländern der Bundesrepublik Deutschland für das Jahr 1991. Gutachten im Auftrage des Bundesministeriums für Verkehr, Berlin.

DIW (1996): Ermittlung der Wegekosten und Wegekostendeckungsgrade des Eisenbahn-, Straßen-, Binnenschiffs- und Luftverkehrs in der Bundesrepublik Deutschland für das Jahr 1994. Gutachten im Auftrage der Deutschen Bahn AG, Berlin.

Dodgson, J.S. (1986): Benefits of Changes in Urban Public Transport Subsidies in Australia, Economic Record 224-235. Reprinted in Glaister, S. (1987): *Transport Subsidy,* Policy Journals, Newbury.

Dorfwirth, Herry (1979): Nutzenkostenuntersuchung im Straßenbau – Berechnung des Mengengerüstes von Straßennetzen, Wien.

DsK (1985): Kostnader och avgifter inom trafiksektorn. Kommunikationsdepartementet. Stockholm 1985.

ECIS (1996): The State of European Infrastructure 1996, Rotterdam.

ECIS (1997): Bottlenecks in European Infrastructure, Rotterdam.

ECMT (1998): Statistical Trends in Transport, Paris (and volumes for previous years).

European Commission (1995): Green Paper "Fair and Efficient Pricing in Transport", Brussels.

EUROSTAT (1983): Stock of Fixed Assets in Industry in the Community Member States: Towards Greater Comparability. *Studies of National Accounts,* No. 2.

EUROSTAT (1996): Eurostat Yearbook '96: A Statistical View on Europe 1985-1995, Luxembourg 1996.

Feeney, B.P. (1987): Allocated Road Infrastructure Costs and Revenue 1987.

Feeney, B.P. (1988): Impact of the EEC System of Road Infrastructure Charging, An Foras Forbartha Teoranta, The National Institute for Physical Planning and Construction Research, Dublin.

Forschungsgesellschaft für Straßen- und Verkehrswesen (1986): RAS-W. Richtlinien für die Anlage von Straßen, Teil: Wirtschaftlichkeitsuntersuchungen, Nr. 115, Köln.

Forschungsgesellschaft für Straßen- und Verkehrswesen (1997): Kommentar zum Entwurf „Empfehlungen für Wirtschaftlichkeitsuntersuchungen an Straßen" (EWS), Aktualisierung der RAS-W'86, Köln 1997.

GVF (1996): Externe Kosten des Verkehrs 1993. *GVF News,* Nr. 36, Bern.

GVK (1982): Schlussbericht der Kommission zur Überprüfung der Strassenrechnung, Bern.

Haavisto, J. (1997): Road Cost Account for Heavy Goods Vehicles in Europe, Helsinki.

Hansson, L. (1993): Traffic User Charges in Swedish Policy, University of Lund.

Hansson, L. (1996): Kostnadsansvaret för trafikens externa effekter - En jämförelse mellan vägtrafik och tågtrafik, The International Institute for Industrial Environmental Economics at Lund University, Lund.

HCM (1950): Highway Capacity Mannual. Bureau of Public Roads. 1st edition. Washington, D.C.

HCM (1965). Highway Capacity Mannual. Highway Research Board. 2nd edition. Washington, D.C.

HCM (1985). Highway Capacity Mannual. Transportation Research Board, Special Report 209. Washington, D.C.

Herry M., Faller P., Metelka M. and Van der Bellen A. (1993): Wegekostenrechnung für die Verkehrsträger Strasse in Österreich, Wien.

Herry M., IPE, Kessel + Partner (1997): Analyse und Prognose des Güterverkehrs in Österreich, Wien.

Heusch/Boesefeldt (1996): Ermittlung der Pkw- und Kfz-Jahresfahrleistungen 1993 auf allen Straßen in der Bundesrepublik Deutschland. Gutachten im Auftrage des Bundesministeriums für Verkehr. Aachen.

Highway Research Board (1961): The AASHO-Road-Test - History and Description of Project, Special Report 61 A, Washington D.C.

Holocher, K.H. (1988): Wegerechnungen für Strassen. *Giessener Studien zur Transportwirtschaft und Kommunikation,* Giessen.

INFRAS (1998): Congestion Costs in Switzerland, Zürich (in progress).

INFRAS (1996): Infrastructure Costs and Revenues in EUR 17, Paper prepared for the ECMT Task Force on Social Cost of Transport, Zurich.

INFRAS (1997): Reduktionspotentiale beim motorisierten Strassenverkehr.

INFRAS, HERRY, PROGNOS (1994): Einzel- und gesamtwirtschaftliche Wege-kostenrechnung Strasse/Schiene in Österreich und der Schweiz, Zürich/Wien/Basel.

INFRAS, IWW (1994): External Effects of Transport. On behalf of UIC, Zürich/Karlsruhe/ Paris.

International Energy Agency (1997): Energy Prices and Taxes, Third Quarter, OECD.

IOO (1995): The Price of Mobility in the Netherlands in 1990, Den Haag.

IOO (1996): De prijs van mobiliteit in 1993, Den Haag.

IRF (1998): World Road Statistics '98, Geneva (and volumes for previous years).

Kommission der Europäischen Gemeinschaften (1969): Bericht über die Muster-untersuchung gemäß Artikel 3 der Entscheidung des Rates Nr. 65/270 EWG vom 13. Mai 1965, SEK (69) 700 endg., Brüssel.

Kommunikationsdepartmentet (1987): Den tunga vägtrafikens kostnader. Ds K 1987:11, Allmänna Förlaget, Stockholm.

LT Consultants Ltd.: Cost Coverage of Road Traffic in Different Vehicle Categories (published only in Finnish: Tieliikenteen ajoneuvoryhmittäinen kustannusvastaavuus.)

Lützel, H. (1971): Das reproduzierbare Anlagevermögen in Preisen von 1962. *Wirtschaft und Statistik (WISTA)*, Heft 10/1971.

Lützel, H. (1979): Reproduzierbares Anlagevermögen nach Wirtschaftsbereichen. *Wirtschaft und Statistik (WISTA)*, Heft 6/1979.

Mayeres, I., Ochelen, S. and Proost, S. (1996): The Marginal External Costs of Urban Transport. *Transportation Research D: Transport and the Environment 1D*, pp.111-130.

McKinsey & Co. (1986): Afrekenen met files, Amsterdam, The Netherlands.

Ministère des communications et de l'infrastructure (1995): Statistique des transport en Belgique, 26 ème edition, Bruxelles (and volumes for previous years).

Ministerio de Fomento: Carreteras Planificacion Recomendaciones, Para la Evaluacion Economica, Coste-Beneficio des Estudios y Proyectos de Carreteras

Ministerio de Obras Publicas, Transportes y Medio Ambiente (1994): Balance Contable de la Carretera: Documento Sintesis Direccion General de Carreteras.

Ministry of Transport (1968): Road Track Costs HMSO, London.

Ministry of Transport (1992): Danish Highway Investment Evaluation Model, Updated 1994/95.

Monzon de Caceres, A., Villanueva Gredilla, J. (1995): Assessment of Congestion Costs in Madrid (Spain). *PTRC,* pp.197-208.

MOTC (1996): Inventory of Assets in the Purview of the Ministry of Transport and Communications.

NEA (1989): Study of Road Infrastructure Costs Applicable to Heavy Goods Vehicles in the European Community, Project for the EC/DGVII, Rijkswijk.

NEA (1997): Filekosten Op Het Nederlandse Hoofdwegennet in 1996, Rijswijk.

NEI (1993): De lasten van de kosten - Effecten van doorberekening van infrastructuur- en externe kosten aan het goederenvervoer, On behalf of Ministerie van Verkeer en Waterstaat - Directoraat-General voor het Vervoer, Rotterdam.

NERA (1997 a): The Costs of Road Congestion in Great Britain: a NERA Briefing Paper by John Dodgson and Barnaby Lane, London.

NERA (1997 b): Motors or Modems? A Report for the RAC, London.

Nordquist, Stig (1958): Gators och vägars kapacitet.

O'Mahoney, M., Kirwan, K.J., and McGrath, S. (1997): Modelling the Internalization of External Costs of Transport: Transport Research Record No. 1576, Transport Research Board, Dublin, pp. 93-98.

PROGNOS (1988): Alternative Methods for Calculating Harmonized Vehicle Taxes, Project for the EC/DGVII, Basle.

PROGNOS (1996 a): Wegeausgabenrechnung 1993 für Deutschland nach Verkehrsträgern - Bericht, in Zusammenarbeit mit dem Institut für Verkehrssystemplanung der TU Wien im Auftrag des Bundesministeriums für Verkehr, Basel.

PROGNOS (1996 b): Wegeausgaben in Deutschland 1994 - Ergebnisband, im Auftrag des Bundesministeriums für Verkehr, Basel.

Ricci, Roberto (1984): La Tariffazione per L'Uso delle Infrastructure Stradali. Ministerio Trasporti, Roma.

SAMPLAN (1995): Översyn av samhällsekonomiska kalkylvärden för den nationella trafikplaneringen 1994 - 1998, Stockholm.

Scheltes, W., Mulder, M. and van Zwam, H. (1987): Costs of Traffic Jams on the Netherlands Main Road Network, Transportation Research Forum, San Antonio, Texas.

Schierhackl, Glaser (1995): Staukosten in Österreich – Abschätzung der einzel- und gesamtwirtschaftlichen Belastungen, Wien.

Schmidt, L. (1992): Reproduzierbares Anlagevermögen 1950 bis 1992. *Wirtschaft und Statistik (WISTA),* Heft 2/1992.

Schmuck, A., Ressel, W. (1994): Wirtschaftlichkeitsvergleich für unterschiedliche Bauweisen, Untersuchungsbericht im Auftrag der European Asphalt Pavement Association, München.

Secretary of Transportation (1982): Final Report on the Federal Highway Cost Allocation Study - Report on the Secretary of Transportation to the United States Congress, Washington D.C.

Snizek et al. (1988) Snizek S., Steierwald G., Steinbach J., Pöschl F., Stottmeister V., Schlosser F., Fußeis W.,: Anforderungs- und Leistungsprofile von Straßen (ALS), Wien .

SOU 89:15: Storstadstrafik 2 - bakgrundsmaterial (Big citie's traffic part 2 - background material). Ministry of Communications. Stockholm 1989.

Statistisches Bundesamt (1997): Statistisches Jahrbuch für das Ausland 1996, Wiesbaden.

Sumpf (1997): Abschätzung der volkswirtschaftlichen Verluste durch Stau im Straßenverkehr, BMW Verkehr und Umwelt.

T&E, Kageson, P. (1993): Getting the Prices Right - A European Scheme for Making Transport Pay its True Costs, European Federation for Transport and Environment.

Tengblad, Å. (1993): National Wealth and Stocks of Fixed Assets in Sweden 1981 - 1990. *The Review of Income and Wealth,* Series 39, No. 2, pp.159-175.

Tengblad, Å., Westerlund, N. (1976): Capital Stock and Capital Consumption Estimates by Industries in the Swedish National Accounts. *The Review of Income and Wealth,* Series 22, No. 4, pp.331-344.

Turvey, R., Anderson, D. (1977): Electricity Economics, published for the World Bank, The John Hopkins University Press, Baltimore/London.

TRANSEK (1990) Gunnar Lind and Esbjörn Lindquist; Avgifter i trafiksystemen (User-charges in transport systems).

Treasury, H.M.: Resource Accounting Manual.

Vejdirektoratet (1994): Oversigt over vejudgifterne i 1994, Danemark.

Vejdirektoratet (1995): Tal om vejtrafik 1995, Danemark.

Project team

DIW, Germany (project leader)

Heike Link (project coordinator, project leader DIW)
Katja Grunow
Barbara Linder
Karl-Heinz Pieper
Heilwig Rieke
Martin Schmied

INFRAS, Switzerland

Markus Maibach (project leader INFRAS)
Silvia Banfi
Christoph Schreyer

Consultancy Dr. Herry, Austria

Max Herry (project leader HERRY)
Susanne Judmayr
Norbert Sedlacek

NERA, United Kingdom

John Dodgson (project leader NERA, NERA London)
James Cameron (NERA, London)
Sarah Evans (NERA, London)
José Maria Rodriguez (NERA, Madrid)

Technical editing and layout: Anja Spahn (DIW)

Contributions to Economics

Hagen Bobzin
Indivisibilities
1998. ISBN 3-7908-1123-8

Helmut Wagner (Ed.)
Current Issues in Monetary Economics
1998. ISBN 3-7908-1127-0

Peter Michaelis/Frank Stähler (Eds.)
**Recent Policy Issues in Environmental
and Resource Economics**
1998. ISBN 3-7908-1137-8

Jessica de Wolff
The Political Economy of Fiscal Decisions
1998. ISBN 3-7908-1130-0

Georg Bol/Gholamreza Nakhaeizadeh/
Karl-Heinz Vollmer (Eds.)
**Risk Measurements, Econometrics
and Neural Networks**
1998. ISBN 3-7908-1152-1

Joachim Winter
Investment and Exit Decisions at the Plant Level
1998. ISBN 3-7908-1154-8

Bernd Meyer
Intertemporal Asset Pricing
1999. ISBN 3-7908-1159-9

Uwe Walz
Dynamics of Regional Integration
1999. ISBN 3-7908-1185-8

Michael Carlberg
European Monetary Union
1999. ISBN 3-7908-1191-2

Giovanni Galizzi/Luciano Venturini (Eds.)
**Vertical Relationships and Coordination
in the Food System**
1999. ISBN 3-7908-1192-0

Gustav A. Horn/Wolfgang Scheremet/Rudolf Zwiener
Wages and the Euro
1999. ISBN 3-7908-1199-8

Dirk Willer
**The Development of Equity Capital Markets
in Transition Economies**
1999. ISBN 3-7908-1198-X

Karl Matthias Weber
**Innovation Diffusion and Political Control
of Energy Technologies**
1999. ISBN 3-7908-1205-6